DRESSING
FUN

__Mum & Dad__

My first (maybe last?!) effort!
Lots of LOVE!

Terry

DRESSING-UP FUN

Terry Burrows

Illustrated by Paul Dewhurst

BEAVER BOOKS

A Beaver Book
Published by Arrow Books Limited
62–5 Chandos Place, London WC2N 4NW
An imprint of Century Hutchinson Ltd

London Melbourne Sydney Auckland
Johannesburg and agencies throughout the world

First published 1989

Text © Terry Burrows 1989
Illustrations © Paul Dewhurst 1989

This book is sold subject to the condition that it shall not, by way of trade or otherwise, be lent, resold, hired out, or otherwise circulated without the publisher's prior consent in any form of binding or cover other than that in which it is published and without a similar condition including this condition being imposed on the subsequent purchaser.

Made and printed in Great Britain
by Courier International Ltd
Tiptree, Essex

ISBN 0 09 965110 6

CONTENTS

Introduction   7

Basic Techniques
Sewing   8
Decorating fabrics   14
Applying make-up   20
Making masks   24
Making 3-D objects   28

Familiar Characters
Asian Clown   32
Chimney sweep   36
Punk   42
Queen and princess   52
Clown   61

The Wild West
Cowboy   71
North American Indian   77

The Space Age
Robot   95
Dalek   102

Superheroes
Batman, Robin and Catwoman   107
Superman and Supergirl   113
Spiderman   114

World of Sorcery
Witch 115
Wizard 126
Ghost 128

Monsters and Villains
Frankenstein monster 131
Dracula 135

Bizarre Notions
Banana 137
Empire State Building 139

INTRODUCTION

Almost from the very beginning, people have dressed up, swapping one role for another with a change of clothing and sometimes with the application of make-up. Today, many people have to wear special clothing, or a uniform, for work. Think of the people you see in real life and on television — policemen, soldiers, nurses, doctors, judges and clowns. Would you like to know what it feels like to be one of these people?

All you have to do is imagine that you are one of them: simply dress as they do and play-act their roles. Similarly, you can pretend to be a boy or girl from another culture or another age simply by kitting yourself out with a sari or an American Indian costume for instance. You'll be amazed at how different you feel! It's even more fun if you get together with a few friends and put on your own play or have a fancy-dress party. Perhaps you could become involved in your school play.

Whatever your reasons for dressing up, you'll find it much more satisfying to make your own clothes and accessories, rather than buying them ready-made. And that's where this book will come in very handy. Full of exciting and unusual ideas, *Dressing-up Fun* shows you how to make all sorts of outfits using common, everyday things that don't cost much or which you should be able to find at home.

Although making your own costumes is great fun, it can take quite a lot of time if you're starting from scratch, so for nearly every project I've included short cuts on converting existing garments. Ask your mum or dad for any discarded old clothes and scour jumble sales for some really cheap clothing. Other good sources of clothing are charity shops such as Oxfam. If you buy your materials from one of these shops, you will also be contributing to a useful cause.

Dressing-up Fun not only shows you how to create many different outfits, it also provides other ideas. Do not be afraid to try out your own designs – for instance, if you think you can make a better robot head than the one shown on page 100, then go ahead and do it! Be creative and, above all, have fun!

BASIC TECHNIQUES

All the clothes in this book are straightforward to make, but before you start, it is a good idea to become familiar with a few basic techniques. With some understanding of sewing, painting fabrics, applying make-up, making masks, and making three-dimensional objects, you will have no trouble making anything in the book.

Sewing

The bare necessities

Although you don't need very much equipment to begin sewing — a needle and thread, scissors, and of course, the fabric — there are some other useful items that can make things easier. Here's a complete list of sewing tools:

Needles — You can buy these in packets that contain a range of different sizes.
Pins — These are useful for joining fabric pieces together temporarily while you do your stitching.
Thread — Usually known as 'cotton', this is what you use to sew the fabric together.
Scissors — There are several types of scissors, each with a particular function. *Dressmakers' scissors* are long, thin scissors for cutting out fabric. But be warned, if you cut card or paper with them, they'll soon become blunt! *Household scissors* are for cutting card and paper. *Pinking shears* have zigzag blades. Use them for cutting thin materials very neatly so that the edges don't fray.

Tape measure – You'll need this to measure the fabric.

Tailors' chalk – This is a special kind of chalk used for drawing on fabric. It can easily be brushed off. A soft pencil (at least 2B) makes a good substitute.

Thimble – Put one of these on the middle finger of the hand holding the needle, so that you can push the needle through the fabric more easily.

Needle threader – This device helps you thread needles.

Unpicker – This is a simple tool for taking out stitches, and is especially useful if you are adapting a lot of old garments, which will probably need taking apart first.

Some basic stitches

There are many different kinds of stitch you can use but you need to know only a couple to make dressing-up clothes – a stitch for joining two pieces of fabric together strongly, and one for sewing hems (the edges of clothes).

Running stitch

To join one piece of fabric to another, the best stitch to use is running stitch.

1. Pin the two pieces of fabric together.

2. Hold the fabric between the thumb and index finger of the hand that will not be holding the needle, and

insert the needle from the underside of the fabric towards you. Pull the needle until the thread is stopped by the knotted end. (Do not pull too hard or the material may become bunched, or the needle unthreaded!)

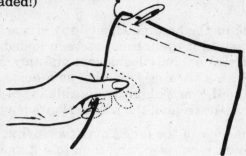

3. Pass the needle back through the fabric about 4mm (⅛ in) along. Congratulations! You've just made your first running stitch!

4. Continue making stitches of equal length until you reach the end of the fabric you are joining. Remember that while it may take longer to make short stitches, they make a much stronger seam.

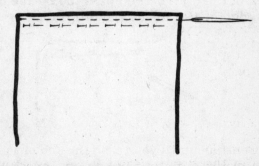

5. When you reach the end of the fabric, make three or four stitches within the space of only a few millimetres. This stops the stitching coming undone.

6. Trim the thread with the dressmakers' scissors, leaving only a couple of millimetres of cotton showing.

7. Remove the pins.

Hem stitch

Take a look at the bottom edge of any of your clothes and you'll see that the fabric has been folded back so that the bottom not only looks neat and tidy, but does not fray. Such a turning is known as a hem. If it has been sewn well, you will hardly be able to see the hem stitches from the front of the fabric. Here's how to do it.

1. Fold the edge of the fabric over twice: first fold the rough edge back on itself, and then fold it again until the fabric is the correct length. Carefully pin the hem in place.

2. Make the first stitch by passing a needle and thread in and out of the edge of the fold that is visible and pulling it until the thread is stopped by the knot.

3. This is the difficult bit! To the left of your first stitch, pass the needle through a few threads only of the main body, of the fabric. Then pass the needle back through the edge of the folded band of fabric.

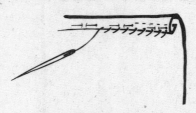

4. Continue until you reach the end of the hem. Finish with a few stitches close to one another to make it secure (see p. 11).

5. Remove the pins.

Sewing machines

Up until fifty years ago, hand stitching was the normal method of sewing clothes. Nowadays, of course, many households have a sewing machine which can perform these functions much more quickly and accurately.

If you have access to a sewing machine, and a bit of help from an adult, you, too, will be able to work much more quickly.

Patterns

The best way of cutting out fabric is to follow a pattern. All clothes can be made from a pattern. You can buy lots of different, ready-made patterns in a haberdashery shop. They are drawn on large sheets of thin paper that show exactly what shapes are needed to make up the garments, and how to sew them together.

Using a ready-made pattern

1. Decide which sections you need.

2. Carefully cut them out, according to the instructions on the pattern.

3. Pin the paper pattern in position on the fabric. Keep the pieces as close together as possible to avoid unnecessary waste. However, make sure that you lay them the right way up *and* facing the right direction. Check, too, whether you should be cutting one or two layers of material. In some cases, you can fold the material, and cut out the front and back using a single pattern.

4. Cut out the fabric, making sure that you don't move it. If you do, the fabric may bunch up, causing you to cut out the wrong shape. This can be an expensive mistake!

Making your own pattern

You could, of course, make your own paper patterns – like some I've suggested in the book. Newspaper is good for this purpose, although if you are working with very light fabrics, there is a danger of marking them with newspaper print. Be especially careful not to move the pattern when cutting out the fabric as newspaper will tear very easily around the pin holes.

Decorating fabrics

There are two main ways of decorating fabric: painting and dyeing. Painting is for creating a specific design or pattern on a surface, and dyeing is for altering the colour of a piece of fabric completely.

Painting shapes

Painting on fabric requires the use of special fabric paints. Before you start, though, it's important to make a few preparations. First of all, make sure that, whether you're working on the floor or a table, it's well protected, as you won't be very popular with your parents if you get paint all over the table or carpet! Large polythene sheets are best for covering surfaces because liquids cannot penetrate them, but newspaper will protect surfaces from the odd splash of paint.

Unless you're very confident of your painting ability, it's always best to work out your design first. You can either draw out the shapes on the fabric directly, or make up a template or stencil to use over and over again. If you draw on the fabric, make sure that you use a very soft pencil (at least 2B), or you won't be able to see the lines. If you're drawing on a dark-coloured fabric, use tailors' chalk (see p. 10). If you make a mistake, you can rub it out simply by wetting a small piece of cloth and dabbing at the marks you want to remove.

Making a template

It's much safer to use a template than to draw your design directly on to the fabric. A template is a piece of cardboard cut to the shape you require. Simply place it on the fabric and draw around the outside edge. Templates are especially useful if you wish to reproduce the same shape a number of times. They're really easy to make, too.

1. Find a piece of card (an old washing-powder box folded flat will do, if it is big enough).

2. Draw your shape on the card (if you make a mistake now, you can erase it with an ordinary rubber, or find another piece of card and start again).

3. Cut around the shape with a pair of household scissors.

4. Now test it out: place the template on a piece of scrap paper and draw around it.

5. If the shape looks correct, place the template on the fabric, move it around until it's in the right place, and carefully draw around the outside with a soft pencil (or tailors' chalk). Continue reproducing the shape until your design is complete. Then fill in the shapes with fabric paints.

Applying the paint

If you are painting a T-shirt or other double-sided garment, make sure that you pad out the area directly beneath the surface you are painting. If you don't do this, thinner fabric paints may penetrate right through to the other side of the shirt. A few sheets of folded newspaper will do, or better still, an old magazine.

It's best to use two brushes, one thin (6mm/¼in) and one thick (12mm/½in).

1. Paint around the edge of the shape with the thin brush, following the lines carefully. Take care not to put too much paint on the brush or you may smudge the outline.

2. Using the thicker brush, paint inside the painted outline. Leave the paint to dry for a few hours.

Fixing the paint

Most fabric paints require what is known as 'fixing', although you can get some that are self-fixing. Look at the manufacturer's instructions to see if you need to fix the paint you are using. This process is really important. If the paint is not fixed and the fabric is washed or gets wet in the rain, the paint will start to come off. This will not only annoy you because you will have wasted lots of time, but it can also be very messy!

Fixing processes differ from one brand to another, so make sure that you read the instructions on the fabric paint very carefully. Generally, though, the technique is as follows:

1. When the paint is dry, cover the surface with a cloth.

2. Place a hot iron on it for a few seconds. You may have to ask an adult for some help, here.

Dyeing

The process of dyeing dates back many thousands of years. Originally, natural substances like berries or fruits were used. You probably know how well blackberry juice stains! Nowadays, dyeing fabrics is fairly straightforward: dyes come ready made in powder or liquid form and are available from most department stores. It can be *very* messy though! So take care.

There are two basic types of dye: hot-water and cold-water dye. As a general rule, you use cold-water dyes with natural fibres and hot-water dyes with synthetic fibres. However, as with all paints and dyes, read the manufacturer's instructions carefully before you begin. The cold-water dyes are the easiest and safest to use. Hot-water dyes tend to be less predictable – the colours sometimes run when they're washed.

There are a couple of things to remember before dyeing fabric:

1. Best results are achieved by dyeing light-coloured garments a dark colour. You can't really do it the other way around, for example, dye black fabric yellow. To do this you would first have to bleach the fabric.

2. It's best to wash newly dyed garments separately as some of the dye is almost certain to come out and affect other clothes in the same wash.

Using a cold-water dye

1. Before you can decide how many tins of dye and dye fixer you need, you must weigh the fabric. The size of the bowl you need also depends on how much fabric is to be dyed. It must be big enough to allow for the whole of the fabric to be submerged all of the time.

2. Fill the bowl with water, and add the tins of dye and the fixer. Put on rubber gloves and stir the mixture slowly.

3. Carefully submerge the garment in the bowl and continue to stir slowly. Leave it for however many minutes or hours are stated in the dye instructions.

4. Take the fabric from the bowl and rinse it thoroughly. It's a good idea to leave it soaking overnight.

5. Once no more dye can be rinsed out, simply dry the garment and it's ready to wear.

Tie-dying

An interesting dye effect is created by tie-dyeing, especially useful if you are dressing as a punk (see p. 42).

1. Tie several very tight knots in the fabric with pieces of cord that will be resistant to the dye (eg, nylon thread or thick elastic bands).

2. Dye the fabric in the usual way (see above).

3. Leave it to dry, then undo the knots. The fabric covered by the cord will not be dyed, revealing some very interesting, swirling patterns.

Transfer printing

Another method of decorating fabrics is to use transfer printing. This is a technique using special transfer crayons or inks. A design is drawn with the crayons on a sheet of ordinary paper. Then the paper is placed face down on top of a piece of fabric and ironed. The design is then transferred on to the fabric.

Transfer printing is especially useful for bold, multi-coloured designs. However, its use is best kept to man-made fibres, as if natural fabrics are used, the colours will often come out very pale.

Making a transfer print

1. Draw your design on a piece of ordinary paper. It's best to begin by getting the design absolutely right before wasting any of your transfer crayons or ink.

2. When you're happy with the design, draw over it using the crayons. Leave the design to dry for a while (as always, check the manufacturer's instructions before doing this).

3. Place the design face down on the fabric.

4. With the iron set at medium, carefully iron the back of the design. Take care that you apply pressure evenly, so that the colours come out looking the same, and also take care not to move the design or this will cause a smudge. (Always remember to ask an adult before you use an iron, since you can very easily burn yourself or cause unnecessary damage.)

5. Take the paper away. The design will have been transferred to the fabric.

6. Leave it to dry.

Applying make-up

A valuable art in dressing up is the ability to change the look of your face. This is usually achieved by using make-up: either proper stage make-up, or the kind your mother or sister buys.

The principles of using make-up are easy to follow, but applying make-up properly requires a lot of skill.

The art of making up is much easier to master once you have understood the effect of making light and dark contrasting areas on your face. Look at your face in a mirror — it's always vital to put on make-up in front of a mirror — and see how strong light exaggerates the contours of your face. If you move around slowly, you'll see that the light highlights and shadows different areas.

It's good, if possible, to start with a 'base': a light-coloured, creamy foundation that will provide a good surface for you to work on — a bit like an artist working on a blank canvas! The base should cover your whole face, right up to the hair line, and down to where your neck disappears into your shirt or jumper.

Quite a few realistic natural effects can be made by applying make-up. Here are a few basic ideas:

Ageing

1. On top of the foundation, apply some pale beige or grey powder to the cheeks. Make sure that you rub it in around the edges, so that it blends in with the rest of your face.

2. Old people's faces have lots of visible lines. To copy them, screw up your face tightly, and draw along the lines lightly with a black or grey eyebrow or eye-shadow pencil. Rub your finger along the lines to soften the effect and make the lines look more natural.

3. Use a darker pencil to draw two curving lines on either side of your nose down to your chin. If you draw them thinly and shade the outer edges of the lines with a thicker pencil, you will create the impression of sagging skin.

4. Cover your face with a light-coloured face powder to hold the make-up in place.

5. To produce a grey-haired effect, take a handful of talcum powder (or flour) and work it into your hair.

Cuts and bruises

Cuts can be created with brown and red eye-shadow pencils.

1. Draw the cut thickly with the red pencil, fading it at the edges to give the impression of sore skin surrounding the cut.

2. Using the brown pencil, draw a thin line down the middle to create the illusion of a scab.

Scars with stitches, for example those on a Frankenstein monster, can be made by taking a thin brown eyebrow pencil and drawing a straight line where you want the scar to be. For the stitches, draw several marks crossing this line, with a black pencil.

To make a black eye or some bruises:

1. Take a black eyebrow pencil and draw around the 'bruised' area.

2. Rub your finger around the edges to make it blend into the rest of the skin.

Moustaches and beards

Moustaches and beards of all types can be drawn on with eye-shadow pencils. Take a look at anyone with a moustache or beard to see exactly how they can be drawn. Make sure that the colour of the moustache or beard is as near as possible to that of the hair. Beards and moustaches can be made to look more realistic by sticking on cotton wool or twists of wool.

Making masks and hats

Masks have been used in plays almost as long as plays have existed. They are very useful especially when you're trying to create a really dramatic look that cannot easily be achieved with make-up. A mask is literally a false face that you wear on top of your own. It can cover just your eyes or your whole head.

Simple masks

The simplest kind of mask can be made from paper or thin card and held on the head with elastic.

Making a cardboard face mask

1. Draw a full-size face on the card. Make it as colourful as you want (see the section on make-up on p. 20 for some ideas).

2. Cut out the face.

3. Make holes for the eyes and mouth. For the nose hole, cut along the sides and bottom of the drawn-on nose, and then poke it out from the back, so that the nose flap hangs from the top and still covers your own nose.

4. Make a tiny hole on either side of the mask just above where the ears will be. Thread some elastic through one hole and knot it in place. Then stretch it to the other hole and knot it securely.

More difficult masks

Papier mâché is a French term which, literally translated, means 'chewed paper'! It is the art of making sturdy objects from paper pulp, that is paper that has been soaked, left to dry, and treated.

Papier mâché is especially good for making masks. You will need a large working surface, such as a big table. It is a very messy technique (what fun things aren't?), so be sure to cover the surface with a protective layer. A large polythene sheet is best, but you could tear open some old plastic shopping bags or bin-liners and lay them out so that they overlap and cover the surface.

Making a papier mâché face mask

Here's a technique that will ensure that the mask you make will fit perfectly. All you need, in addition to some newspaper and paste, is a piece of cooking foil and a thick piece of card, both about 30cm (1ft) square.

1. Take the cooking foil and place it over your face. Now press your hands firmly around the contours of your face. Be particularly careful that you don't push too hard at the eyes: apart from tearing the foil, you might just give yourself a nasty poke as well!

2. Take the foil away. It should contain an imprint of your face. Measure about 12mm (½in) from the edges of the foil mask and bend up this margin all the way around.

3. Lay the mask on the card and tape the flattened edges to it.

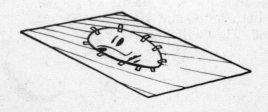

4. Mix some wallpaper paste in a bucket or washing-up bowl. The ingredients of these pastes differ greatly, so, as always, be sure to follow the manufacturer's instructions on the back of the packet. If you haven't any paste, a mixture of flour and water will do the trick, although it won't be as strong.

5. Tear some newspaper into pieces no larger than about 25mm (1in) square – the pieces don't have to be exactly the same dimensions.

6. Put on a pair of rubber gloves (unless you want really sticky hands!), take a piece of newspaper and dip it in the paste. When it is thoroughly soaked, stick the paper to the top of the foil.

7. Build up the thickness of the mask by placing layer upon layer of pasted paper over the shape. Do not press down too hard or you may damage the contours of your face.

8. When you have built up between five and ten layers of paper, leave the mask to dry overnight.

9. Continue building up the mask. When you have finished and it is completely dry, make holes for the nostrils, eyes, and, if necessary, the mouth. You can now decorate it as you like (see the section on make-up on p. 20).

10. Make small holes on either side of the mask just above the ears. Thread a piece of elastic through both holes and knot either end. This will keep the mask on.

Making a papier-mâché head mask

One of the great advantages of using papier mâché is that it is very easy to build up surfaces with it. You could, for example, make a mask that covers your entire head by using a balloon, and building up the contours of the face with papier mâché: this technique works really well for animal or monster masks.

1. Take an inflated balloon and draw a line around it from top to bottom and back again. Build up five layers of newspaper on one side only and let it dry.

2. With a felt-tip pen, draw a face on the front, particularly noting where the contours will fall, eg, the eyebrows, cheek-bones, and chin.

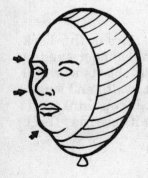

3. Slowly build up these particular areas, using smaller pieces of paper. This is a bit like sculpting with clay or Plasticine. Here is a profile of what the mask should look like after a few layers of paper.

4. If you wish to build out a long way, fix an object to the mask, and paper over it. For example, if you are making a dog's mask, glue a paper cup to the surface and cover that with paper, instead of building up a 75mm- (3in-) long nose, layer by layer.

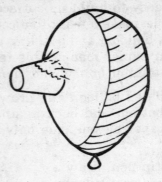

5. Tidy up the edges of the mask by cutting a neat edge all the way around with a pair of household scissors.

Making 3-D objects

In order to make some of the accessories in this book, such as hats and helmets, a reasonable understanding of making three-dimensional, or 3-D, objects is useful.

A 3-D object is one that has height, width and length, like, for example, a box or a sphere. If you think about it, virtually everything you can see is three-dimensional.

Boxes

If you follow the example below of how to make a box 50mm (2in) square, you'll soon understand how to make a 3-D object out of a single piece of card.

Making a cardboard box

1. Take a piece of plain card and draw a ruled line down the middle from top to bottom. Take a ruler and mark the card at 50mm (2in) intervals on both sides of the line across the top and bottom of the page.

2. Turn the card around and join the lines up like this:

3. Mark out the following areas:

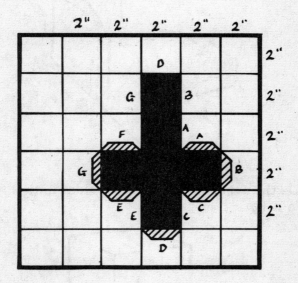

If you were to cut out the black shaded area and fold the card into squares, you would find that all the edges joined up to make a box. However, in order to join the edges together you must add flaps to your design. These are indicated in the diagram by the diagonally shaded areas.

4. Cut around the whole shape, including the flaps. Fold the squares and the flaps along the lines. Now apply some glue to flap A. Fold the card and fix it behind the side marked A. The box should now look like this:

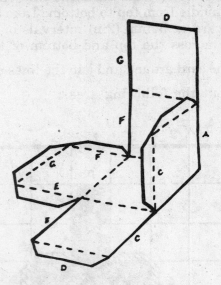

5. Do the same for all the other sides until you have made a box.

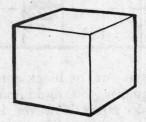

Any shape, with the exception of a sphere – a ball shape, which should be made with papier mâché (see below) – can be made using this technique.

Helmets

Rounded, three-dimensional or highly textured objects, such as an astronaut's helmet are straightforward to make with papier mâché.

Making a papier mâché helmet

1. Take a balloon and blow it up until it's just a bit larger than your head. Knot it so that it doesn't deflate.

2. With a felt-tip pen, draw a line horizontally all the way around the balloon, about half-way down, in the shape you want the edge of the helmet to be.

3. Stick pasted strips of paper to the balloon as for the face mask (see p. 25) until you have completed a single layer that covers the whole of the top of the balloon down to the line you have made.

4. Continue building up layers of paper until you have between five and ten layers. Then leave it to dry overnight.

5. The next day continue until you've built up between fifteen and twenty layers of paper. The structure should now be solid enough to use. When it's completely dry, take a pin and burst the balloon. You are now holding the basic helmet.

6. You will, most likely, be left with fairly ragged edges, so carefully cut a neat edge all the way around with a pair of household scissors. To build up a lip around the edges, simply add more strips of papier mâché that fold *around* the edges.

7. When the helmet is completely dry, paint it using watercolour paints. To make it more sturdy, finish it off with a coat of polyurethane varnish.

FAMILIAR CHARACTERS

Throughout the years many of us have enjoyed entertaining ourselves and others by dressing up and assuming the roles of familiar characters. Here are some easy-to-make costume suggestions for a few of the most enjoyable of them: including a clown, a chimney sweep, and a queen or princess. There are, of course, many others that you could try out, for example, the doctor and the nurse.

Asian

The traditional garment worn by an Asian woman is a sari. This is, quite simply, a dress made out of one long piece of thin cotton fabric, and is often very brightly coloured.

The female **Asian look** consists of a sari, a choli (short blouse), and bangles.
The male **Asian look** consists of a thin white cotton suit and a turban.

Sari

The great thing about making a sari is that there is hardly any complicated work for you to do: you're just wrapping yourself up in one big piece of cloth!

You will need:
Tape measure
Fabric *about* 372cm (13ft) long (this will vary according to your height)
Thin cloth belt or waist petticoat
Needle and thread
Sequins/diamante (optional)

1. Measure from your belly-button down to your ankles. This measurement is the width of the fabric you need.

2. Take one end of the fabric and fold about 5cm (2in) behind the belt or petticoat. Wrap the whole thing — in an anti-clockwise direction — around your body once, so it gives the effect of a skirt. Tuck in the fabric as you go.

3. Wrap the material around again, this time making pleats and tucking them into the belt.

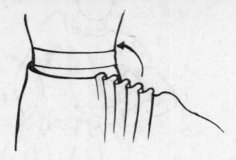

4. Take the remaining fabric, bring it under your arm, over your other shoulder, and let it hang down your back. If it hangs down too far, it will probably get really dirty, or, worse still, you could trip over it! So ask someone to make a mark at about waist length, so that you can cut the extra piece off and stitch a hem neatly (see p. 12).

On particularly hot days, the sari is often worn with the hanging end covering the head, like a head-scarf, to protect it from the sun.

The hanging ends of the sari are often very brightly decorated in shiny threads. Why not sew on some small sequins or diamante, for additional effect! This can be really spectacular in the sunlight!

Choli

The choli is a thin, tight-fitting blouse.

> *You will need:*
> T-shirt
> Scissors
> Needle and thread

1. Cut an old T-shirt to a few inches above the bellybutton.

2. Sew the hem (see p. 12).

Turban

For the Asian male, the most well-known garment is the turban. This is a sort of hat that is made by wrapping a long piece of thin cotton. Being able to do this properly takes a lot of practice as it is a really complex set of procedures. Here, however, is a more simplified version. Again, it's really simple to do because all you have to do is wrap it around your head!

> *You will need:*
> Old white bed sheet   Scissors

1. Cut off a piece from the side of the sheet measuring about 60cm (2ft) wide. Fold it into quarters lengthways to produce a piece of fabric about 240cm (8ft) × 15cm (6in).

2. Take one end of the material and hold it against your forehead so that about 20cm (8in) hangs down in front of your face.

3. With one hand holding this end, take the rest of the material and wrap it around and around your head. Start above the eyes and ears and gradually move upwards, creating a layered effect.

4. When you cannot wrap it any further, tuck the remainder in at the back.

5. Take the length hanging at the front, pull it up straight and tuck it in the top at the front.

For a more colourful effect, some Asian men wrap a brightly coloured band of thin cloth around their forehead before wrapping on the turban. When the turban is fixed in place, one straight edge of the coloured material can be seen. This might be a sort of Asian equivalent to a tie!

Chimney sweep

If you've ever seen the film *Mary Poppins*, you'll know the famous scene in which lots of dirty, grimy chimney sweeps dance their way across the rooftops. Nowadays, of course, it's quite a respectable job, and all the dirty work is done with machines. But you can still have great fun creating the old look for a fancy-dress party. It's really quite easy to achieve, too.

The whole appearance should be really dirty and grimy, but this can be achieved without you having to be dirty yourself! (Unless, of course, you want to be really authentic!)

> **The chimney-sweep look:**
> well-worn top hat
> jacket and trousers
> chimney-sweep's brush
> soot-encrusted face and hands
> accessories

Hat

A good hat for an old-fashioned chimney sweep is a broken top hat. The same hat can double up as a tramp's hat if you like.

If you can get hold of a very old top hat, just bash it about until it's completely misshapen and there you have it. However, top hats are not easy to find these days, so you'll be *very* lucky to find one. Here's how to make one:

You will need:
Cardboard
Ruler
Pencil
Scissors
Paperclips
Glue
Black paint
Paintbrush
Sticky tape

1. Mark out on the card a rectangle measuring 30cm (1ft) × 40cm (16in).

2. Carefully cut it out.

3. Draw the two shorter sides together.

4. Position the tube on your head, holding the sides together. Adjust it so that the sides overlap and the tube sits on your head comfortably.

5. Place a paperclip at the top and bottom of the overlapped sides to keep it in place. Glue the edges together.

6. Draw and cut out a circular piece of card 30cm (1ft) in diameter. Stand the tube in the centre of the circle and carefully draw around it. Draw another circle about 25mm (1in) inside this circle and cut it out.

7. Make cuts from the centre of the circle to the inner line at intervals of 12mm (½in). Bend the segments upwards.

8. Place the tube over the folded segments to check that it fits. Then put a touch of glue on each segment, and attach them, one by one, to the tube.

9. All that's left to make now is the top of the top hat, which should be barely fixed on, like a flapping lid, or fixed so that it points upwards. Take another piece of card and place it on the top end of the tube. Turn it upside-down and draw around it. Before you cut it out, draw a tab protruding from the circle 25mm (1in) long × 12mm (½in) wide. Cut it out and bend down the tab.

10. Paint the inside and outside of the hat black.

11. Now glue the lid on by the tab, so it can flap open.

12. To make the lid sit up at an angle, unfold a paperclip, bend it in the middle to the correct angle, and tape it to the inside of the lid and stem of the hat.

Jacket and trousers

What you really need here is an old black suit. If you can't get one, you could dye a grey suit black (see p.17). (What better use for an old school uniform!) Once you have a black suit, all you really need to do is make it look a bit shabby.

You will need:
Old jacket and trousers
Scissors or unpicker
Black tie

1. Turn the suit inside out.

2. Using scissors or an unpicker, pick away a few stitches up the arms, around the collar of the jacket, and around the hems in the trousers.

3. Pull the thread until you tear away a few inches more. You could even cut off the cuffs and turn-ups leaving frayed edges.

Brush

A long, tall brush was used to sweep out chimneys. If you don't want to make one there is a short cut (see below).

You will need:
Card
Pencil
Scissors
Some 3mm- (⅛in-) thick wire
Glue
Nail
Hammer
Broom handle

1. Take the card and draw two circles 7.5cm (3in) in diameter. Cut them out.

2. Cut the wire into twelve 45cm (18in) lengths.

3. Spread glue on one of the pieces of card. Lay out the pieces of wire on the card to make a brush-head like the one shown in step 5. Let them dry for a while.

4. Put some glue on to the other piece of card and press if firmly to the other side of the wires.

5. Take a small nail and hammer it through the circle to the end of the broom handle. You may need to ask an adult to help you do this.

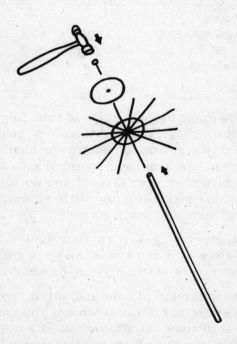

6. Paint the whole brush black.

Short cut

An alternative to making a proper chimney-sweep's brush would, of course, be simply to use an ordinary kitchen broom – nearly every household has one of these. Make sure, though, that it's an old-fashioned wooden broom. They didn't have plastic brooms in those days!

Make-up and accessories

To produce the dirty face and hands, black stage make-up is best.

You will need.
Black stage make-up
  or soil
Flour *or* talcum
  powder
Flower
Scissors

---

1. Apply the make-up to the tips of your fingers, and lightly rub it over your face, neck and forehead. If you do not have any make-up, dampen your hands, go out into the garden and rub them in some soil, and then rub that lightly over your face. If you do this, make sure you haven't picked up any little stones, because they could give you a nasty scratch!

2. To complete the look, rub your hands together thoroughly after applying the make-up or soil to your face, as if you were washing your hands.

3. Now take a handful of flour and smear it over your clothes – it's best to do this outside if you don't want a lot of mess to clear up afterwards. If you can't get hold of any flour, use talcum powder, but make sure it's not your mum's best beforehand, though!

4. A nice finishing touch is to place a pretty flower – a rose or carnation – in the button hole on the jacket. If the jacket doesn't have one, just take a pair of scissors and make a 12mm (½in) slit in the left-hand lapel.

Punk

The punk look that came about at the end of the 1970s, in one way or another, dominated fashion for many years. Its after-effects can still be seen. The punk rock look says 'Anything goes!' It's a really good way of using old clothes that would otherwise be thrown away.

The punk look:
torn T-shirt
bin-liner trousers or
    dress
studded belt
spiked hair
earring/nosering
wild make-up

T-shirt

To make a punk T-shirt, all you have to do is take a really old T-shirt and make lots of big tears in it. It is really good fun!

> *You will need:*
> T-shirt
> Scissors
> Safety pins
> Fabric paint *or* dyes
> Ink

1. Make a small hole in the T-shirt with a pair of scissors, and then pull hard on each side of the cut. Make sure that you are not using one of your best T-shirts, though!

2. Pin the cut material together with some big safety pins.

3. Enhance the whole effect by ripping off the collar and cuffs. Then make big splodges on the T-shirt using fabric paint, dye, or even good old-fashioned ink.

Bin-liner clothes

Bin-liners – the black plastic bags that the dustmen leave for you to fill with rubbish – are really good for the punk look, be it for trousers or a dress. These clothes are incredibly easy to make, and the great thing about them is that the more rough-and-ready your clothes, the better!

Making trousers

You will need:
2 bin-liners
Pair of jeans
Scissors
Reel of sticky tape,
5cm (2in) wide

1. Open out the bin-liners along the bottom and edges until you have two flat pieces of black polythene.

2. Take a pair of jeans and lay them on top of one of the binliners, *very* roughly cut around them, making sure that you allow 5cm (2in) to 7.5cm (3in) extra width around the edges. Do the same with the other bin-liner.

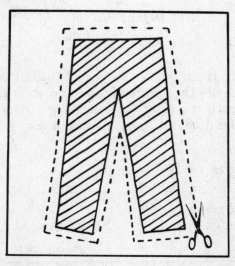

3. Now, instead of stitching the material together like a proper pair of trousers, simply lay one piece on top of the other and wrap sticky tape around the edges. Don't worry about crinkling the plastic up — it all adds to the effect!

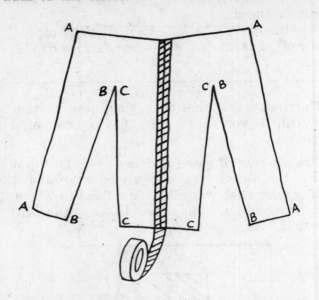

4. Now try them on. If they are too loose anywhere, simply take another piece of tape and stick the offending area until it's tight. Instead of wearing a belt or braces to hold them up, use some sticky tape!

Making the dress

You will need:
Bin-liner
Scissors
Sticky tape
Belt

1. Hold the bin-liner so that the open end is at the bottom.

2. Using the scissors, cut a hole in the middle at the top for the neck, and one on each side near the top for the arms.

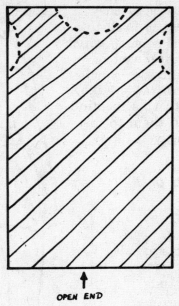

OPEN END

3. You've just made a dress! You can shorten the length by cutting as much as you like off the bottom. If you want to tidy up the collar and cuffs, just wrap tape around the edges! Bring it in at the waist by wearing a belt (see below).

Studded belt

Studded leather belts are a popular part of the punk look. As well as wearing a belt around your waist, you can wear it around your neck, arms or legs! Belts are readily available, but they can be very expensive. Here are a few cheap alternatives that you can make.

The studs that fix to the belts can be bought at upholstery, or haberdashery shops. They are very easy to use: the stud is fixed to a pair of straight prongs, which you open out after you've passed them through a hole in the material, rather like split pins. With this in mind, you can attach them to just about anything you like!

Converting a belt

You will need:
Old black plastic belt
Skewer
Upholstery studs

1. Mark on the belt the pattern you want to make with the studs. If the belt is wide enough, you could even spell out your name in studs.

2. Using a skewer, carefully make small holes along the outline of the pattern.

3. Take a stud, pass the prongs from the outside of the belt, through the hole, and open them out at the back so that they lie flat.

4. Repeat with each stud until you've finished making the pattern.

Making a new belt

If you haven't got an old belt you can use, you can easily make a tie-up belt from a piece of black fabric.

> *You will need:*
> Tape measure
> Black fabric
> Upholstery studs
> Needle and thread
> (optional)

1. Measure your waist. Take a piece of black fabric 30cm (1ft) longer than that, and about 7.5cm (3in) wide. You can sew up the hems if you like (see p. 12), but remember, neatness isn't very important for the punk look.

2. Mark where you want the studs to go. Don't put any on the last 15cm (6in) of each end or tying a knot will be difficult!

3. Fix the studs on as before.

4. To wear the belt, instead of threading it through a buckle, simply tie it up in a knot.

Another amusing alternative if you are small is to go into a pet shop and buy a large dog collar. This can then be worn around your neck!

Hair

Spikes

The punk look usually means having spiky hair. There are numerous setting gels or mousses available that, if applied in large quantities, will hold your hair in place. If you have long hair and want to mould it into something bizarre, apply a mixture of sugar and water which should hold it in place.

Colour

It's also possible to buy brightly coloured hair dyes that will wash out after only a few rinses. You'd better check that it's OK with your parents before you do this, though!

If you use dyes *be absolutely sure* to follow the manufacturer's instructions. It's also a good idea to have an old towel handy: some dyes can ruin your parents' best towels, not to mention the carpet!

Finishing touches

Wild face make-up is popular among punks (male *and* female): very pale (or white) foundation, lots of very thick black eye-liner, unusual-coloured lipsticks and mascara (especially black), and painted symbols. You

could even write your name, that way everyone will know who you are!

The safety pin

One of the first objects to symbolize the punk look was the good old-fashioned safety pin. This can be used in all kinds of ways.

Earrings – Many earrings have tiny loops from which the decoration hangs. Why not remove what's hanging there, and replace it with a big safety-pin? You don't need pierced ears to wear earrings. You can buy clip-on earrings to which you can glue anything at all. Ask your mother if she has any old earrings you can adapt.

Necklace – Make a daisy chain of safety pins by looping them together.

Badge – Just fix safety pins to your clothes and wear them like badges.

Wrap-around sunglasses

Sunglasses that wrap around your face and are almost impossible to see through are very popular with punks.

Queens and princesses

There is as much interest in queens and princesses today as there has ever been. Royalty features heavily in traditional stories and almost every famous fairy story (even modern ones like 'Star Wars') involves a beautiful princess. Here are some ideas for dressing up as elegantly as a queen or a princess, perhaps like Sleeping Beauty or Snow White.

The queen or princess look:
long shiny dress with puffed out sleeves
crown or a headdress
lots of jewellery

The dress

A royal dress should be a really elegant, long, flowing robe with full, puffed-up sleeves. If you don't want to make one you could convert an adult's dress (see p. 55).

> *You will need:*
> Tape measure Tailors' chalk
> Piece of shiny fabric, Pins
>   120cm (4ft) × 180cm Scissors
>   (6ft) Needle and thread

The dress should be made in two sections: the main dress and the sleeves.

Making the main dress

1. Measure yourself around the chest.

2. Measure yourself from the shoulder to the ground.

3. Add 5cm (2in) to each of these measurements.

4. Fold the material in half, right sides together, so that it appears as a rectangle 120cm (4ft) × 90cm (3ft). Mark out this pattern using tailors' chalk:

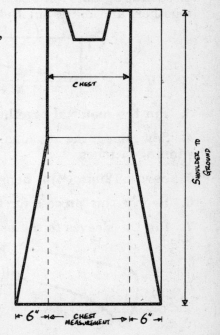

5. Pin the material together a few centimetres inside the line, and cut out the shape.

6. Sew carefully along the line using small, neat running stitches (see p. 10). Stop sewing about 15cm (6in) from the top of each side. This is to allow the sleeves to be sewn on.

7. Sew a 12mm (½in) hem (see p. 12) around the bottom of the dress and the collar.

Making the sleeves

1. Measure the distance from your shoulder, down your arm, to your knuckles. (This will allow for the cuff to be turned up.)

2. Once again, fold some material, right sides together, and mark out the following shape:

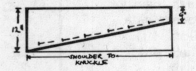

3. Pin the material together and cut out the shape.

4. Sew along the diagonal edge using small, neat running stitches.

5. Sew a 12mm (½in) hem around the cuff.

6. Repeat this process for the other sleeve.

7. Pin the sleeves to the body of the dress as shown:

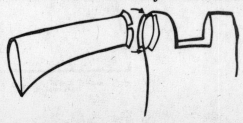

8. Sew on the sleeves using a running stitch.

9. If necessary, sew up the sides of the dress to the points where the sleeves begin.

10. Turn the whole dress the right side out, and try it on.

Converting an adult's dress

You could, of course, try converting an adult's dress. It will obviously be too big for you, but if you tie it up at the waist with a belt or a piece of shiny material cut into the shape of a belt, the puffed-up effect will be even more impressive. Remember, though, always to ask permission before you play around in your mother's best dress.

The crown

No queen worth her salt would be seen without her ceremonial crown.

You will need:
Tape measure
Thin card
Ruler
Pencil
Scissors
Compass
Glue
Paperclip
Gold paint *or* tin foil *or* metallic wrapping paper
Paintbrush
Plasticine

1. Measure around your head directly above your ears. Add an extra few centimetres to this measurement (to allow for gluing the overlap).

2. Take a piece of card, and mark up a rectangle the length you've measured above and 7.5cm (3in) wide.

3. Cut out the rectangle.

4. Mark it up like this:

Create the curves by marking off 5cm (2in) intervals along the top, and drawing semi-circles with the compass set to 25mm (1in).

5. Cut out the shape, fold it round so the edges meet, and glue the overlap. Use a paperclip to hold it in place until it's dry.

6. Paint the crown with gold paint, or cover it with tin foil, or gold-coloured wrapping paper.

7. For that finishing touch, roll some very small balls of Plasticine and place them on the tips of the crown.

8. If you have any small pieces of coloured metallic wrapping paper, cut out small jewel shapes, and glue them to the side of the crown.

The pointed hat

This sort of hat is never worn these days. It is a long pointed conical shape with a long ribbon attached to the end of it — and must rate as one of the least practical hats ever worn!

> *You will need:*
> Thin card
> Pencil
> Compass
> Scissors
> Glue
> Paperclip
> Shiny material
> Ribbon

1. Take the card and, using a compass, mark out a quarter-circle with a radius of 30cm (1ft).

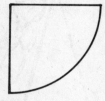

2. Cut out the shape.

3. Bend it around so that the edges meet and overlap very slightly.

4. Glue the edges and hold them in place with a paperclip.

5. Place the cone on your head. It will undoubtedly be much too big, so make a mark on the outside where your ears reach, and draw a line evenly around the cone. Cut along the line and discard the extra card.

6. Wrap the wimple in shiny material. When the wimple is covered, cut out the material and then glue it to the wimple to cover it completely.

7. Make a 25mm (1in) vertical slit at the top of the hat, and thread through three or four ribbons 30cm (1ft) long. Tie a knot in each of them inside the hat, so they don't pull out. The wimple is now complete.

Jewellery

Some of the most beautiful and extravagant jewellery ever made has been designed for queens and princesses. Here are some ideas for making your own slightly cheaper jewellery.

Pearl necklace

This beautiful pearl necklace (not using real pearls, of course!) will be 180cm (6ft) long. This gives you plenty of room to wrap it around your neck several times.

> *You will need:*
> Thick thread, 180cm (6ft) long
> Necklace clasp
> Thin fuse wire
> Nail and piece of wood
> Plastic 'pearls'

1. Fold the thread in half. Attach the necklace clasp with a little knot to one end of the thread.

2. Wrap a piece of fuse wire tightly around the first centimetre of the thread (from the clasp). This will make the clasp more secure.

3. Slip the clasp over a nail on a piece of wood, and pull the thread tightly.

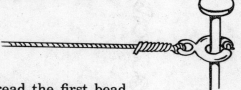

4. Thread the first bead.

5. Tie a knot in the thread. Pull the two strands of the thread apart so as to tie the knot as tightly to the bead as possible.

6. Continue threading the beads and knotting the thread until you reach the end.

7. Tie the other end of the catch on, and wrap some fuse wire around the thread to secure it.

Earrings

You could make similar jewels for hanging from an earring (or clip-on earring base). Simply cut out the 'jewels' as you did for the brooch. This time, however, cut out two identical shapes for each jewel. Instead of fixing them to cardboard, glue the backs of the identical shapes to each other, sandwiching a thin piece of cotton thread between them. Then glue the top 'jewel' to the earring base.

Other accessories

There are many other accessories that you could make for your own royal occasions, such as using the flip-tops of drink cans as rings. Look at some images of royalty through the ages – real or fictitious – for more ideas.

Of course, instead of making your own accessories, you could always ask your mum or big sister if they'll let you play with their *real* jewellery. Never do this without asking first, though – you're not going to be very popular if you lose your mum's best necklace!

Clown

The circus clown has been with us now for over 200 years, yet, during all that time, the look has remained unchanged: the outsize clothes, the funny hat, the colourful make-up are still with us. So here's your chance to turn your house into a three-ring circus and entertain your family and friends!

The clown look
baggy trousers
braces
colourful top
pointed hat
false nose
big shoes
colourful make-up
jokes

Baggy Trousers and Braces

The most notable thing about the clown's baggy trousers is that the waistband does not come in at the waist — the trousers are actually held up by a pair of braces.

There are two ways of making the trousers: making a simple pair from scratch; or converting a pair of adult pyjamas, which can be quicker (see p. 65).

Making your own clown trousers

As these trousers are deliberately silly, you don't have to worry too much about making a normal pattern, which can be quite intricate. All you need is a front and a back to sew together!

You will need:
Light-coloured fabric	Fabric paint
Pair of your jeans	Needle and thread
Pins	Stiff wire
Tailors' chalk	Sticky tape
Scissors	Thick cord

1. Take a piece of fabric that, when folded in half, is big enough for you to lay out a pair of your own jeans, with about 15cm (6in) to spare. Pin the fabric together.

2. Using tailors' chalk, draw around your jeans, about 15cm (6in) wider than the edges. Cut along the line. You will now have two identical pieces of fabric.

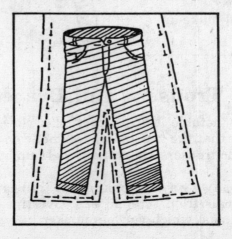

3. Unpin the fabric. If you want to paint or decorate the fabric, it's best to do this right now. Big, bright red spots make a good decoration. Print them on using a halved potato dipped in paint. You could also use the appliqué technique, cutting out some spots from old offcuts of material, and gluing or sewing them in place.

4. Lay the two pieces of cut-out material on top of one another, wrong sides together. In this way, when the trousers are folded out at the end, they will appear the right sides out. Pin them together as shown.

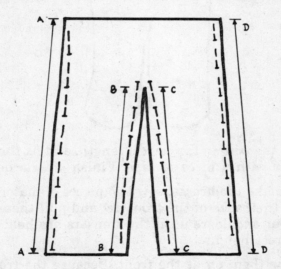

5. Sew running stitches (see p. 10) along the lines A-A, B-B, C-C and D-D as shown.

6. Take out the pins, turn the trousers the right side out, and try them on for size. They should be really big. Roll up the legs until they're about 7.5cm (3in) above your ankles. Take off the trousers, and mark where they are to be turned up. Cut them off about

25mm (1in) below that mark and sew up the hems on each leg (see p. 12).

7. Now sew the hem around the waist, leaving a gap unstitched. Take a piece of stiff wire the exact length of the waistband, and thread it through the hem until it comes out the other end.

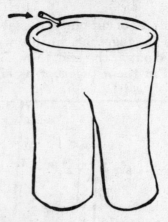

8. Cut the wire to the correct length, and fix the ends together with a piece of tape. Finish off the hem.

9. To make the braces, sew two pieces of material or cord to the backs of the trousers, and pull them both over your shoulders until the trousers are held up to the correct height.

10. Sew them on at the front. Because the trousers are so roomy, you should be able to do this while you're still wearing them.

11. A good short-cut to making your own braces is to get hold of 2 brightly coloured ties and attach them to the trousers in the same way. If you want to use the ties again, you needn't sew them, just fix them with safety pins.

Converting adult pyjamas

You will need:
An old pair of adult pyjamas
Scissors
Needle and thread
Stiff wire
Sticky tape

1. Try them on for size, then mark where they need to be cut off around the waist and ankles.

2. Follow the instructions for making your own trousers. The only modification you may have to make (depending on whose pyjamas you're using) is to sew up the fly area, which is easily done with a running stitch (see p. 10).

Hat

The traditional clown hat is a long, pointed cone shape with a furry ball (or pompom) on top.

You will need:
Cardboard
Ruler
Pencil
Compass
Scissors
Paint, felt-tip pens, or crayons
Glue
Wool
Needle and thread
Sticky tape

Making the cone

1. Take a piece of thin card and draw a line 40cm (16in) long, near to one edge. Make a mark exactly at the halfway point, that is, 20cm (8in) along.

2. Set your compass to a radius of 20cm (8in). Draw a semi-circle from the centre point.

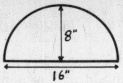

3. If you don't have a compass, or if the one you have is too small, it's not too hard to create a makeshift compass from a pin, a piece of string and a pencil. Simply take a 25cm (10in) piece of string, and tie it around the bottom of the pencil. Measure and mark 20cm (8in) along the string from the tip of the pencil. Take the pin and fix it through the string to the centre-point mark on the card. Draw a semi-circle with the string stretched at all times.

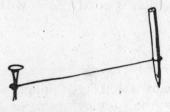

4. Cut out the semi-circle.

5. Draw the sides together so that they overlap.

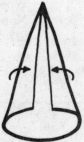

6. Holding the sides carefully in place (it may be easier to hold it together with a paperclip) position the cone on your head to see if it fits. If it's too big, overlap the edges further, if it's too small overlap them less.

7. When the hat is comfortable, take it off and mark the extent of the overlap. Rule it off to the centre of the cone.

8. Before gluing the seam, it's a good idea to do any drawing or painting on the hat as it's always easier on a flat surface. Try painting spots, stars or smiling faces. And add glitter to make the hat sparkle. To do this, put down a thin layer of glue where you want to put the glitter and pour lots of glitter on top. Leave for a few minutes to dry, and then tip the excess glitter back into the packet.

9. When you're happy with your design, apply glue to the edge of one side of the card. Draw it around again until it reaches the overlap line, and hold the edges together until they are dry.

Making the pompom

The only thing missing from the hat is the pompom ball at the top. To make one of these, all you need is some thin card, wool and a needle with a big enough eye to thread the wool through. If you don't want to make a pompom, there is a short cut (see overleaf).

1. On a piece of thin card draw a circle 7.5cm (3in) across. From the same point, draw another circle 25mm (1in) across. Cut around both lines to leave a 'Polo'-shaped piece of card.

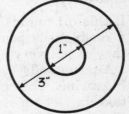

2. Thread the needle with the wool, and loop the wool around the card once, knotting the loop in place.

3. Continue looping the wool through the hole, working around the card evenly, and keeping the loops of wool tightly packed. Carry on doing this until you have been around the card so many 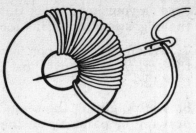 times that the hole in the middle is almost filled in.

4. Now pass the needle and wool through the sausage of wool threads as many times as you can to secure, all the while pulling tightly. Leave about 15cm (6in) of wool hanging.

5. Take the 15cm (6in) length of wool and tie it to another piece of wool close to the card.

6. Cut the wool threads around the edge of the circle. Cut away the card and ruffle the threads. The pompom is complete.

7. Fix the pompom to the tip of the hat either by sewing it in place, or by passing the loose wool thread down inside the hat, pulling tight, and gluing it inside.

Short cut

If this all sounds too difficult, you could always buy a ready-made pompom from a haberdashery shop — they're not very expensive.

Alternatively, you could make a pompom out of Plasticine. This can look especially effective if you take a lot of small pieces of different-coloured Plasticine and roll them together in the palms of your hands. Roll up a ball about 2.5cm (1in) in diameter, and press it firmly over the end of the hat.

Shoes

Clowns usually wear brightly coloured shoes that are many sizes too big for them. Shoes are very difficult to make, so the best thing you can do here is to see if you can get hold of an old pair of adult tennis, or canvas, shoes. Tennis shoes are good because as they're white, you can easily paint them, and, as they are made from canvas, you can decorate them with thick, waterproof, felt-tip pens.

You will need:
Old pair of adult shoes
Newspaper
Felt-tip pens
Brightly decorated shoe laces

To solve the problem of the shoes being too big for you, simply screw up some old newspaper and push it right down into the toes. Then try them on for size: if they're still too big, put in more old newspaper.

Decorate the shoes using felt-tip pens. For added colour, replace the laces with multi-coloured ones.

Make-up

The finishing touch to the clown look is the make-up.

You will need:
Scissors
Table-tennis ball
Red paint
Make-up
Sticky tape

The nose

A false red nose is a traditional device, and, while you can buy one readily from a joke shop, it is also easy to make one out of an old table-tennis ball.

1. Make a small hole in the plastic ball with a pair of household scissors.

2. Slot it over your nose. If it's uncomfortable, make the hole bigger; if it's too sharp, wrap some small pieces of tape around the edges. Paint it red.

Clown face

When it comes to painting your face, you're limited only by your own imagination (and the make-up you have, of course). To make a traditional clown face, you really need white face paint and red lipstick. It's useful to have someone else to help you – which can also be good fun!

1. Completely cover your face with the white paint. This provides the basis of the look.

2. Decide whether you want to be a happy clown or a sad clown. Then take the red lipstick and draw a large exaggerated mouth, either smiling or frowning, around your own mouth.

3. Draw big diamond shapes around the eyes.

You do not have to create the traditional look. Try making two great big rosy cheeks, or painting polka dots or use a multi-coloured make-up stick (obtainable from toy shops) for some interesting effects. A make-up stick is marvellous fun, as, when you run it across your face, you create loads of brightly coloured lines. WARNING: some types of make-up can be a bit difficult to get off (so you may have to use special removal creams). Some may also affect people with very sensitive skin, so it's best to try them out on your arm first. As always, do make sure you read the manufacturer's instructions.

THE WILD WEST

The looks of the characters from the wild west are based on all those old westerns that they keep showing on television, where the cowboys spend all their time chasing Indians and shooting each other. Dressing up in wild west style has not only been popular with children for many years, but many wild west clubs exist throughout the world where *adults* enjoy dressing this way, too!

Cowboy

The real cowboys lived in North America during the last half of the nineteenth century and generally behaved no differently from anyone else. Of course, you don't have to be a boy to dress up as a cowboy! In the real 'wild west' there were plenty of famous girls like Annie Oakley, or in the old movies like *Calamity Jane*.

The cowboy look:
stetson hat
tasselled jacket and
 trousers
gun
holster
sheriff's badge

Stetson hat

The article most commonly associated with the cowboy is the hat. Several different kinds of cowboy hat were worn in the wild west, the most common being the stetson, the ten-gallon and the Mexican.

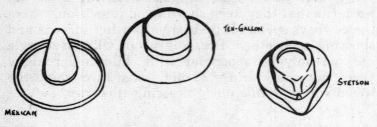

If you don't want to make your own hat, you could always use something like an old trilby hat. You can often find these in second-hand or thrift shops, or your grandfather might have one locked away in his loft.

Making a stetson

You will need:
Cardboard	Glue
Pencil	Brown felt
Compass	Fabric glue
Scissors	Masking tape

1. Take a piece of card and draw a semi-circle with a 25cm (10in) radius. Cut it out and bend it around to make a cone shape.

2. Holding the edges together, place it on your head and adjust the size. Overlap the edges of the cone until it fits over your ears quite comfortably. Remove and mark the position of the overlap.

3. Unroll the card and draw a semi-circle 12cm (5in) in from the outer rim. Cut along this line. Glue the overlapping edges of the semi-circle of card, with the middle cut out, into position to make the cone.

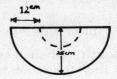

4. Take another piece of card and draw a circle 45cm (18in) in diameter.

5. Take the chopped-off cone and place it in the centre of the circular piece of card. Draw around the bottom.

6. Cut around the inner circle and remove the small circular piece of card. This should leave you with a large circle of card with a hole in the middle. This will make the rim of the hat.

7. Take a piece of the felt, and draw a circle 5cm (2in) larger in diameter than the hole in the top of the chopped cone. Draw another circle inside this the same size as the circular hole. Cut out the larger circle of felt and cut 'V' shapes all around the edge as far down as the inner circle.

8. Place some fabric glue on the back of the outer circle ring of felt with the 'V' shaped cut-outs. Place the fabric on top of the cone and fold down the flaps so that they stick to the side.

9. Take another piece of felt and fold it around the rest of the cone. When it covers the cone completely, cut out the material and glue it with fabric glue to the cone. The cone should now be completely covered in felt.

10. Repeat for the rim of the hat.

11. From underneath, push the chopped cone through the hole in the circle of card that is the rim. Secure the rim to the central part of the hat by placing 5cm (2in) masking tape over the edges of both parts.

12. Cut and glue another piece of felt to cover the underside of the rim and the tape.

All traditional cowboy hats can be made using the same method. Simply modify the relative sizes of the parts. Try cutting the rim to a different shape or altering the height of the top section.

Tasselled jacket and trousers

Famous western show personalities, like Buffalo Bill or Annie Oakley, often wore tassels on their jackets and trousers. The tassels provided an extra flourish when they drew their guns from their holsters at great speed.

The easiest way to achieve this effect is to modify an existing jacket and pair of trousers: simply open out the seams, insert the tassels, and sew them up again. But if this sounds like too much trouble, there is a short cut you can take (see p. 77).

You will need:
Old jacket and trousers
Tape measure
Cotton fabric
Dressmakers' scissors
Unpicker *or* small pair of scissors
Pins
Needle and thread
Thick cord

---

1. Take the jacket and measure the length of the arm from the shoulder to the cuff. Now take the trousers and measure the leg from the hip to the ankle.

2. Fold the fabric in half. Mark out two rectangles, one the length of the arm measurement by 10cm (4in) wide; the other the length of the leg measurement by 10cm (4in) wide. Pin the fabric together and carefully cut out the rectangles. This will give you four pieces of fabric altogether: two for the arms and two for the legs.

3. To make the tassels, make cuts 7.5cm (3in) deep at intervals of 6mm (¼in) along one side of each of the four rectangles. Take care not to cut too far into the rectangle, and completely cut the material in half!

4. To fit the tassels to the arms, turn the jacket inside out, and using either an unpicker or a small pair of scissors, unpick the seam. You may find that there is a lining in the arms. If so, remove this as well – it's not too important (although a proper tailor – a professional clothes-maker – might disagree on this point!).

5. Take one of the arm strips of tassels and insert it into the seam that you have just opened. Pin so that the tassels are facing inside the sleeve. Make sure the strip is level, so that when you turn the jacket the right way around, the tassels will all appear the same length.

6. Using very fine running stitches (see p. 10), sew the seam back together with the strip sandwiched in between.

7. Repeat for the other arm. Then turn the jacket the right side out.

8. Repeat the process for the trousers. Turn them inside out, unpick the seams, sandwich the strip between each, and sew them back together again.

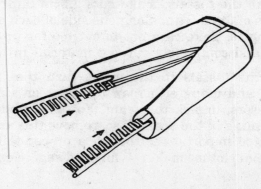

Short cut

A simpler alternative is to take the strips, fold them around a 6mm (¼in) piece of cord, and then stitch the whole thing along the outside of the seam. This avoids the need to unpick them.

1. Fold each strip of fabric around a 6mm (¼in) piece of cord.

2. To stitch around the cord and 'trap' the sleeve and fabric with the tassels in place, start at the shoulder. Making a starting stitch, then pass it *around* the cord and through the strip, about 12mm (½in) along. Continue until you reach the cuff.

North American Indian

The North American Indian is one of the most famous screen images of cinema and television. In actual fact, Hollywood – where the most famous westerns were made – almost entirely rewrote history by portraying 'red' Indians, as they were often called, as violent people, whereas in truth, they normally lived in peace-loving tribes.

That apart, dressing as a red Indian can be great fun, especially on hot summer days.

The red Indian look:
headdress or headband
war paint
loin cloth
skirt
bow and arrow
tomahawk
moccasins
wigwam
totem pole

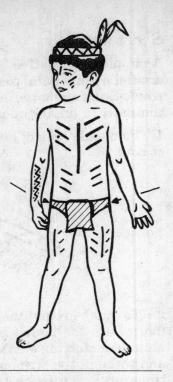

Headdress

The main component of the colourful Indian headdress is the birds' feathers. If you don't live in the country, you will probably have to buy synthetic feathers from a haberdashery shop. If you don't want to make a headdress from scratch, there is a short-cut (see next page).

You will need:
Scissors
White cotton fabric
Ruler
Fabric paints
Paintbrush
Needle and thread
Different-coloured thread
Feathers

1. Cut a 5cm (2in) band of white cotton fabric, 15cm (6in) longer than the circumference of your head.

2. Decorate it with your own design. You might like to try painting with fabric paints (see p. 14) or you could stitch patterns on top with different coloured cotton threads. To do this, draw the patterns directly on the band. Then, using different-coloured threads, sew some very close running stitches (see p. 10) along the lines.

3. Take three or four feathers and stitch them to the inside of the band at the centre of the strip. For additional colour, you could paint the feathers different colours with fabric paints.

4. Position the band around your head and tie it together at the back.

Short cut

A simpler way of doing this is to buy an elasticated head-band — the sort that tennis players often wear. Put it on and poke the feathers inside the band.

War paint

You will need:
Brown, red, black and white stage make-up

1. Cover your face and neck with the brown make-up. This gets the basic skin complexion right (American Indians are dark-skinned).

2. Make patterns using the other colours, and really go to town! Here is a traditional look to try out:

Loin cloth

Originally made from animal skin, the loin cloth looks like an over-large pair of underpants. A ready-made option is to use a suitably coloured pair of swimming trunks (or paint them yourself). However, you can also make a loin cloth very simply from two squares of fabric – choose a pale brown material that looks a bit like animal skin.

You will need:
Tape measure
2 pieces of fabric, about 30cm (1ft) square
Ruler
Scissors
Pins
Needle and thread
String *or* ribbon

1. Measure around your waist. Divide this measurement by two, and subtract 5cm (2in).

2. On each piece of fabric, draw two lines so that they cross in the middle. Each line should measure the length you have worked out. Join the ends of the lines to form a square. Cut the squares out.

3. Fold each square diagonally across, and hold them together so that you appear to have four triangles. Pin together the middle two triangles and stitch the bottom corners together with a few running stitches (see p. 10).

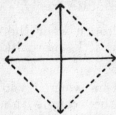

4. Cut out and hem (see p. 12) four 7.5cm- (3in-) long ties. You could use old pieces of ribbon, string or some offcuts of the material. Insert the first tie 25mm (1in) into the fold of one of the triangles at one end. Pin and sew it into place using running stitches (see p. 10). Repeat for each folded corner.

5. Try the cloth on. Simply place one folded triangle at the front, the other through your legs to the back, and knot the ties at each side. As you can see, the middle two triangles act as the 'pants', and the two outer triangles flap quite freely.

6. As a finishing touch, tear the outer triangles to make them look a little more like genuine animal skin.

The loin cloth can be worn if you want to dress as Tarzan or some other jungle inhabitant. Imitation leopard-skin fabric could be especially useful here.

Skirt

A very simple red Indian skirt can be made from a material that looks like animal skin.

You will need:
Tape measure   Elastic
Tailors' chalk   Pins
Fabric   Needle and thread
Scissors

1. Measure around your hips, and also from your waist to just below your knees. Add 5cm (2in) to both measurements.

2. Take some tailors' chalk and mark out, on the wrong side of the material, a rectangle whose length equals the hip measurement, and whose width equals the length measurement. Cut out the material.

3. Measure your waist. Subtract 5cm (2in) from that figure. Cut the elastic to this length.

4. Fold the material in half lengthways and pin together the edges. Sew them up using a neat running stitch (see p. 10).

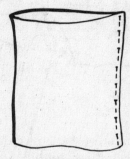

5. Turn over the top 12mm (½in), and sew it up using a hem stitch (see p. 12). Before you reach the end, thread through the piece of elastic. Knot the elastic and finish sewing the hem.

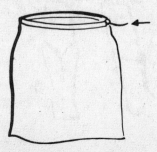

6. Mark off the bottom of the skirt at 25mm (1in) intervals. At each mark, draw a line 15cm (6in) upwards. Carefully cut along all the lines.

7. Turn the whole skirt the right side out and try it on.

Tomahawk

The tomahawk is a special kind of axe and is probably the most famous red Indian weapon. If you don't want to make a tomahawk, there is a short cut (see p. 87).

You will need:
Tubular piece of wood 25mm (1in) in diameter × 30cm (1ft) long
Pencil
Ruler
Fretsaw
File
Piece of wood, 10cm (4in) × 5cm (2in) × 60cm (2ft)
Sandpaper
Silver *or* gun-metal paint
Paintbrush
Wood glue
Strip of ribbon *or* cloth, 90cm (3ft) × 12mm (½in)

The first part of this operation is a little tricky, so you might need some help from an adult.

1. Take the tube of wood and draw a line right around it 5cm (2in) from the end, and another line 25mm (1in) from that.

2. Draw two horizontal lines to link the first two lines together, exactly 12mm (½in) apart.

3. Ask an adult to cut a groove between these horizontal lines. Then cut a 12mm (½in) hole at each end of the groove and take the rest out with a fretsaw and file. That's the handle of the tomahawk complete.

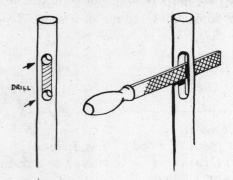

4. Make the blade from the other piece of wood. Mark a line 25mm (1in) from one of the narrow ends, and two lines 12mm (½in) in from each side of the thick edge.

5. Draw two diagonal lines, as shown below. Carefully cut away and leave only the shaded areas:

6. Take some heavy-gauge sandpaper and rub it against the edge of the 'blade'. If you have access to a vice, place the wood in the vice, wide edge up. Wrap a piece of sandpaper over the edge of the wood and, holding it between the thumb and index finger, rub back and forth until the wood gradually comes to a point.

7. To smooth the blade, finish sanding it with a fine-grade sand-paper or glasspaper.

8. Slot the tomahawk 'blade' into the handle. If it doesn't fit, rub away at the 'blade' with the sandpaper until it does so. Don't worry if it's loose: the handle and blade will be glued together.

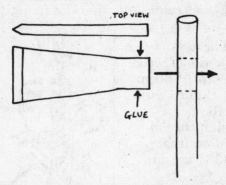

9. For a more authentic appearance, paint the blade silver (or if possible use a special silvery/black colour called 'gun-metal'). When it's dry, apply wood glue to the points shown and press firmly together. Leave it to dry for a few hours.

10. To complete the tomahawk, take one end of the 12mm (½in) ribbon, and glue it to the end of the handle. Wrap it diagonally up and down the bottom of the handle until you've used it up. Glue the end of the ribbon into place.

Short cut

If you think making the tomahawk is too complicated, then there is a much simpler solution which hardly involves any work at all: draw the design of the tomahawk on some thick corrugated cardboard, cut it out and paint it.

Bow and arrow

The bow consists of a straight, springy piece of wood with a strong thread attached to each end, so that when you pull back the thread in the middle, the wood arches.

The idea is to place the arrow against the thread, pull it back and release it, thereby firing the arrow.

You will need:
Flexible piece of wood
   3mm (⅛in) × 60cm
   (2ft) × 12mm (½in)
Small drill
Thick nylon thread
Wooden doweling,
   90cm (3ft) × 6mm
   (¼in)
Fretsaw
Sandpaper
Rubber suckers *or*
   Blu-Tack

Making the bow

There are two crucial points to remember when making the bow. The first is that the wood should be flexible enough to bend and strong enough not to snap. The second point is that the thread should be strong enough not to snap. Use nylon thread, the kind that is often used in gardening.

1. Make a mark in the centre of the wood, 18mm (¾in) from each end, and drill a very small hole (no bigger than 1mm/¹/₁₆in) at each end. You might need the help of an adult with this.

2. Pass the nylon thread through one of the holes and knot it three times.

3. Measure 75cm (2ft 6in) along the thread, pass it through the other hole and tie another three knots. Make sure the thread is left slightly loose.

Making the arrows

A 90cm (3ft) length of 6mm (¼in) wooden doweling will make three arrows.

1. Mark off the rod at 30cm (1ft) intervals and saw across the lines carefully. If the edges are rough, rub some sandpaper around them until they are smooth.

2. Arrows, when fired from a bow, can be *very dangerous*, so it's important to put something on the tips to make them safer. Some model shops sell small suction pads that can be placed safely over the tips, but a good fall-back is to use a lump of Blu-Tack, or some polystyrene.

3. Finally, so that the arrows do not slip off the wire, cut a 6mm (¼in) 'V'-shaped piece out of the ends: the thread will lodge in this nicely!

REMEMBER, EVEN WITH PROTECTIVE TIPS, IT CAN BE DANGEROUS TO POINT OR FIRE AN ARROW AT ANOTHER PERSON OR ANIMAL.

Moccasins

Moccasins are the footwear most commonly associated with red Indians. They were simple shoes made from animal skins. You may already have a pair of moccasin indoor slippers. If you're short of time, you could take an ordinary pair of indoor slippers and paint them using fabric paints. However, here is an example of how to make a pair of your own using some thick canvas. They may not be weather-proof like the originals, but they could easily double as slippers!

You will need:
Thick canvas, about 90cm (3ft) × 60cm (2ft) (if you can't find any canvas, use an old furry blanket)
Tailors' chalk
Scissors
Pins
Thick cardboard
Thick needle and nylon thread

1. Fold the canvas in half to make it thicker. Take some tailors' chalk and draw around both your feet, leaving a gap of 5cm (2in). These pieces will make the sole and sides of the moccasins.

2. Mark out two more similar pieces that have only front halves. These will make the tops of the moccasins.

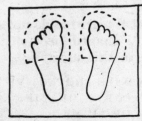

3. Cut out all the pieces. Remember that they are all two layers of material thick, so to make sure that you keep them together, pin them.

4. Mark two 5cm (2in) 'V' shapes in the backs of the soles.

5. Draw around each foot on the piece of card. Cut out the shapes.

6. Place the card for the left foot centrally between the two sole sections so it is sandwiched in the middle. Now fold the front of the sole section upwards, and bunch the canvas up. Hold the bunching in place by sewing a running stitch through it.

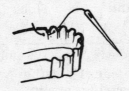

7. Take the top section for the left foot and sew it to the bottom section with a running stitch (see p. 10) about 12mm (½in) in from the top. When you've done this all the way around, the moccasin should look like this:

8. To complete the moccasin, sew up the heel sections to the sides with running stitches, about 12mm (½in) from the edges.

9. Repeat these steps for the right foot.

10. As a finishing touch, decorate the moccasins with zigzags, stripes and circles.

Extras

To accompany dressing as red Indians, why not go a step further and create a few interesting pieces of scenery like wigwams and totem poles?

Making a wigwam

A wigwam is a small tent.

> *You will need:*
> 3 bamboo canes, 150cm (5ft) tall
> String
> Fabric paint
> Thick fabric

1. Tie the three canes together loosely with the string, about 7.5cm (3in) from the end. Now carefully open them out so that they look like three legs of a tripod.

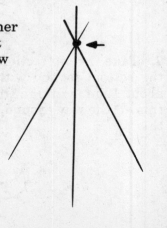

2. Paint the material with Indian symbols.

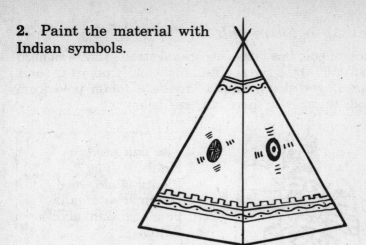

3. Drape the material over the top of the tripod.

4. For a more sophisticated design, measure the triangles made by the poles. Cut out four triangles from the fabric and sew them together with a running stitch. This would provide you with an overlapping piece for the entrance.

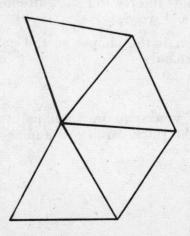

Making a totem pole

A totem pole is a large, decorated statue that was used in rituals. On it the red Indians usually depicted their gods. If you don't want to make a totem pole from wood, there is a short cut (see below).

You will need:
Knife
Plenty of old wood
Hammer and nails
Pole 5cm (2in) across
Paint

1. Cut out some interesting and suitable shapes from the scraps of old wood.

2. Carefully nail the shapes to the pole and paint them bright colours.

Short cut

Alternatively, you could draw and paint a design like this on to some thick cardboard and then cut it out.

THE SPACE AGE

Even though it's barely twenty years since man first landed on the moon, the idea of space travel and the likely technical innovations of the future have captured people's imaginations for many hundreds of years. Even science fiction films made less than fifty years ago predicted that by now man would have conquered numerous planets, have robots to do all their work, and be fighting strange alien creatures from other worlds.

Robot

For many years now, in science fiction books, cartoon strips and big feature films from *The Wizard of Oz* to *Star Wars*, we've seen many different kinds of robot. Here's an exciting and challenging way of dressing up for all kinds of games and fancy-dress parties.

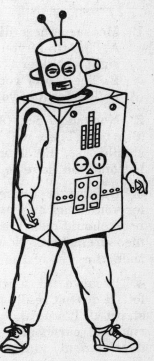

> **The robot look:**
> mechanical body and head
> mechanical hands and feet
> antennae

Body

The body is made of a large cardboard box covered in silver foil. You are unlikely to find a cardboard box that fits you exactly, so first take some measurements. (You will probably need some help to do this – unless you have three arms!)

You will need:
Tape measure	Masking tape
Large cardboard box	Silver foil
Compass	Glue
Pencil	Rag
Scissors	

1. Measure these distances:
   A. The tip of your left shoulder to the tip of your right shoulder.
   B. The top of your shoulder down to your knees.
   C. The front of your head to the back of your head.

2. Now add 7.5cm (3in) to each of A and B and 15cm (6in) to C. These will be the dimensions of the 'box' you should use. Remember that the box won't have a bottom (you have to be able to get into it somehow).

3. Before you cut anything out, mark three holes, one for your head and two for the arms. The hole for the head should measure 5cm (2in) more in diameter than measurement C. Now carefully cut out the holes and then the rest of the 'box' to make these shapes.

4. Because the whole box will be covered in silver foil, it doesn't really matter how neatly the box is constructed. It's unlikely that you'll have a piece of corrugated cardboard big enough to do the whole development, so if you need more card, take sections

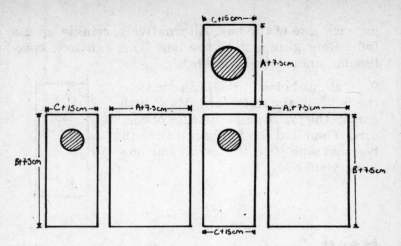

out of an old cardboard box and tape them together using thick masking tape.

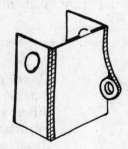

5. Now try the box on for size. If the holes in the arm or head are too small simply make them a bit bigger.

6. All you have to do now is cover it in silver foil. This is easy. First unroll the silver foil against the box. When it covers one side, cut it off the roll.

7. Spread the glue over this side of your box and carefully press the foil on to it.

8. Take an old rag and carefully smooth out the foil. This will get rid of air bubbles and excess glue. Repeat for each side of the box. Alternatively, crinkle up the foil before gluing it to the box. This can look spectacular under bright lights.

9. Cut out holes in the foil to match the holes in the cardboard. Make little cuts in the foil around the edge of the card. Then fold the foil back inside the box and glue it to the card. You now have your body!

Head

The head is made on the same principle as the body, the difference being that you make a cylindrical shape.

You will need:
Tape measure
Pencil
Cardboard
Scissors
Glue
Silver foil
Masking tape
2 paper cups
Silver paint
Paintbrush
Assorted knobs and dials

1. Take the following two measurements:
A. The top of your head down to your shoulder.
B. The circumference of your head (that's how big your head is around the outside).

2. To allow you to put the head on over your nose and ears, add 15cm (6in) to measurement B and draw a circle of this circumference on a piece of card.

3. Mark out a large rectangular piece of card 15cm (6in) longer than measurement B and 15cm (6in) wider than measurement A.

4. Add a 25mm (1in) lip. Mark out the eye and mouth holes. Cut everything out.

5. Before you do any gluing, fold the rectangle around until the edges meet, then put it on your head to check the size. If it's too small, I'm afraid you must have made some incorrect measurements and you'll have to start again. But it's best to find out now, rather than when you've finished it!

6. Construction is simple. Put some glue on the 25mm (1in) lip of the rectangle, and fold it until the edge rests on top of the glued lip. Press down firmly for a few seconds.

7. Take the circle and make some 'V'-shaped cuts into the edge. Make sure that you don't cut in further than 25mm (1in) or you will damage a part that is visible.

8. Press the 'V'-shaped lips down and apply glue to them. Carefully fix them to the inside of the head.

9. Cover the head with silver foil in the same way as the body.

10. Fix the head over the top of the body using 5cm (2in) masking tape.

11. Paint a couple of paper cups silver (or cover them in silver foil) and fix one to each side of the head: this will provide a neat pair of ears!

12. Another nice touch is to take some knobs and radio dials and glue them (or Blu-Tack them) to the side of the head. If you don't have any knobs, why not use tops from things like old toothpaste tubes?

Hands and feet

There are all kinds of things you could use for hands and feet. Here's an idea that uses wellington boots and regular kitchen rubber gloves. Think about what *your* favourite robot looks like.

You will need:
Newspaper
Rubber gloves
Wellington boots
Silver spray paint

---

1. Put down lots of newspaper to protect the work surface.

2. Make sure the room is well ventilated. (If it's a nice day, it's best to do spray painting outside.)

3. Hold the spray about 30cm (1ft) away from the gloves or boots and spray lightly all over.

This kind of paint doesn't usually take too long to dry, but you may need to give it several coats of paint before it's ready.

Finishing touches

What is a robot without all the complicated gadgetry? You can make a lot of gadgets out of old pieces of wire or coat-hangers. Here's an easy way of making antennae to fit on to the robot's head.

Making antennae

> *You will need:*
> Old wire coat-hanger   Blu-Tack
> Pliers

1. Cut the handle off an old wire coat-hanger with a pair of pliers, and straighten it out.

2. Bend the coat-hanger into a 'V' shape, and fix it firmly on the top of the robot's head with Blu-Tack.

3. For a finishing touch, put a few blobs of Blu-Tack, or, better still, some brightly coloured beads, on the ends of the antennae. (Make sure the holes are big enough to go over the wire, though!)

Decorating the body

One interesting idea is to find a mass of old, thin, brightly coloured wire. Tangle it all together and carefully tape it to the front of the body.

Dalek

The Dalek, that old enemy of Doctor Who the famous TV time-traveller, can look really spectacular at a fancy-dress party.

> **The Dalek look:**
> Dalek body
> decorative features
> weapons

The Basic body

> *You will need:*
> Cardboard
> Pencil
> Paperclips
> Glue
> Scissors
> Tape measure
> Compass
> Masking tape, 5cm (2in) wide

1. Wrap a piece of card 75cm (2½ft) × 45cm (18in) around the lower part of your body until the edges overlap. The top should fit loosely around your waist with enough room for you to get your arms down each side easily.

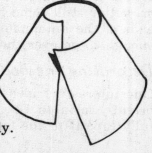

2. Mark where the card overlaps with a pencil, or hold it together with some paperclips.

3. Glue the overlapping edges together. Fix them with a paperclip at each end so they don't move while drying out.

4. Cut the tops and bottoms until they are both straight.

5. Measure from your waist to the top of your head — A. Also, measure the width of the 'waist' section that you made above — B. Add 5cm (2in) to figure B and cut out a rectangular piece of card of these dimensions.

6. Draw a straight line along the bottom edge, 5cm (2in) in from the edge.

7. Score this line. Take a pair of scissors and snip straight lines from the edge up to the line, and fold the tabs outwards.

8. Fold the card around to make a big tube, with the tabs you've just made folded outwards at the bottom. Ensure that the edges of the card overlap to make the tube exactly the same size in diameter as the construction you made in (1). Glue the overlap and hold it in place until it is dry.

9. Apply glue to the tabs, and pass the whole tube through the bottom of the body until it comes out the other end. Press the tabs against the inside edge of the body to make one solid piece.

10. Using a compass, draw a circle on some card the same size as the hole left in the top of the body. Draw another circle around the outside, 25mm (1in) wider. Cut into the edge as far as the inner circle to make small 'V'-shaped tabs.

11. Score, and fold the tabs.

12. Apply some glue to the tabs and stick them to the inside of the top section.

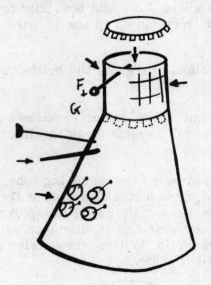

13. You can strengthen this joint by sticking some masking tape around the inside, so that it half overlaps the side and the top.

Decorative features

> *You will need:*
> Paintbrush
> Silver paint *or* silver foil
> Black paint
> Cardboard egg boxes
> Strong glue

Paint the Dalek in the following way:

1. Either paint the whole body silver, or cover it with silver foil. Paint the features at the top with black paint.

2. Among the notable features of the Dalek are the 'bobbles' near the bottom (see [12] above). For this you could either paint on little black circles (in columns of four all the way around), or glue on old cardboard egg boxes.

3. Take an egg box, and cut around each individual holder.

4. Paint them black and, when dry, carefully glue them to the body. Instead of holding each one until it's stuck on firmly, 'pin' each side like this:

Weapons

The Dalek has three weapons (again see [12] above), two at waist height and one on the 'head'. They burst into life shortly after the Dalek shrieks the immortal phrase 'EXTERMINATE! EXTERMINATE!'

The two waist-high weapons can be made so that they can be operated from inside the Dalek.

You will need:
2 wooden dowel rods, about 30cm (1 ft) long
Paintbrush
Silver paint *or* silver foil
Tennis ball *or* Plasticine
Black paint
Scissors
Masking tape
Knitting needle

1. Paint the rods silver, or wrap them in silver foil.

2. On the end of each, place an old tennis ball, painted black. Simply puncture each ball and cut out a hole. Alternatively, take two balls of Plasticine and push them over the ends.

3. To 'install' the weapons, make two holes 25mm (1in) across in the body of the Dalek, and pass the ends of the rods through them. To avoid tearing the card, fold some tape over the edge of the holes.

4. For the weapon on the Dalek's head, make a small hole right at the top of the cardboard head with a knitting needle. Pass the needle through and fix it to the inside of the head with some masking tape.

5. As a finishing touch, take two balls of Plasticine. Spear the first and pass it half-way down the needle. Press the other on to the tip.

SUPERHEROES

The great superheroes are those that have appeared in comic books for years. These are the beings with extraordinary super powers, such as the ability to fly or to catch bullets fired from guns. Dressing up as one of these great characters can be enormous fun for all kinds of games. There are so many of them to choose from, too. Just take a look in any comic.

Batman and Robin

One of the greatest superheroes is Batman, who, with Robin, defends Gotham City (where Batman and Robin live) from those arch-villains, the Joker, Penguin and, of course, Catwoman.

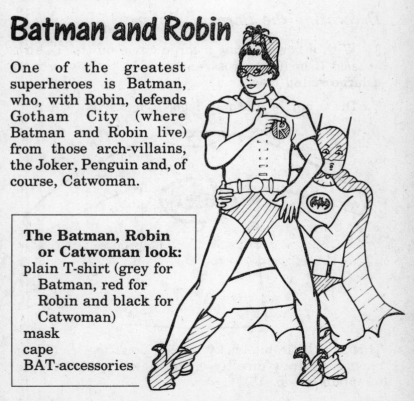

The Batman, Robin or Catwoman look:
plain T-shirt (grey for Batman, red for Robin and black for Catwoman)
mask
cape
BAT-accessories

T-shirts

> *You will need:*
> Pencil
> Grey or red T-shirt
> Paintbrush
> Black/yellow fabric paint *or* material
> Scissors
> Glue
> Needle and thread
> Fasteners

See p. 14 for the basic painting techniques.

Decorating the Batman T-shirt

1. With a pencil, draw a large circle on the T-shirt, at least 15cm (6in) across — it's easiest to draw around a large round object.

2. Draw on the Batman logo. It looks like this:

This is a little bit tricky. If you don't feel confident enough to draw directly on to the shirt, make up a template (see p. 15).

3. For complete accuracy, paint the bat black and the background yellow.

A somewhat cleaner alternative is to use 'appliqué' shapes. For the Batman logo, cut out a circular piece of yellow material and sew or glue it to the T-shirt. Then draw the bat logo on a separate piece of black material. Cut it out and glue or sew it to the circle. Appliquéd shapes have the advantage of washing better, too.

Decorating the Robin T-shirt

Robin's design is a little simpler. It features a small circle on the left breast with a big letter 'R' in the middle. Additionally, Robin has a series of bright yellow fasteners down the front of his shirt.

1. Find something circular to draw around, this time about 7.5cm (3in) across and draw a circle on the left breast of the T-shirt.

2. Draw a big 'R' in the centre of the circle. Again you could make your own 'R' template from card.

3. Paint the T-shirt using fabric paint. Paint the circle background black, and the 'R' shape and fasteners yellow.

Again, the logo can be appliquéd instead of painted, using the technique described above.

Catwoman's top is just a simple black long-sleeved T-shirt, jersey or leotard.

To complete the Catwoman look, ideally you need a pair of tight black leather trousers! Since you may not have these, a good substitute would be a pair of black jeans, or alternatively some thick black woolly tights.

Masks

Making Batman's mask

Batman's mask can be made using papier mâché. Follow the steps for making the helmet (see p. 31) but make sure that it covers the eyes.

You will need:
Balloon
Wallpaper paste *or*
   flour and water
Bucket *or* bowl
Newspaper
Pencil
Scissors
Paintbrush
Black paint

1. Blow up the balloon so that it's a little bit bigger than your head, and mark the basic shape of the mask around it.

2. Create the basic helmet. Gradually build up two 'ear' pieces at each side, until you've produced two pointed ears.

3. Cut out holes for the eyes and paint the whole thing black, then try it on.

Making Robin's mask

Robin's mask is a very simple 'lone ranger'-style mask. This is easy to make from a piece of card and some elastic.

> *You will need:*
> Tape measure
> Cardboard
> Pencil
> Scissors
> Elastic
> Paintbrush
> Black paint

1. Measure the distance across your face. Take a piece of card this wide and 7.5cm (3in) high, and draw out the following shape:

2. Carefully cut out the shape, and cut out holes for the eyes.

3. Make a small hole at either side of the mask and thread through a piece of elastic, long enough to go round the back of your head. Knot it at each end to secure.

4. Finally, paint the mask black.

Catwoman's mask is made in the same way as Robin's mask, the only difference is the shape. Catwoman's should be pointed to emulate the pointed ears of a Siamese cat.

Cloak

> *You will need:*
> Cotton fabric
> Dark grey *or* yellow dye
> Safety pin *or* brooch

Both Batman and Robin wear cloaks. All you need to do is take a large piece of cotton fabric, dye it dark grey (Batman's cloak) or yellow (Robin's cloak), let it dry, then wrap it around your neck and secure it at the front with a safety pin or brooch.

There are, of course, many other superheroes you could dress up as. Here are a few ideas. Their looks can be achieved by adopting the same techniques as above.

Superman or Supergirl

The famous Superman look can easily be converted to his female counterpart — the costume is uni-sex.

The Superman or Supergirl look:
blue T-shirt with the Superman symbol
red cloak
blue trousers
red boots (painted wellington boots)
cloak
mask

Spiderman

> The Spiderman look consists of a red T-shirt with the spider pattern on it, a spider mask (made either from papier mâché or simply from card), and a cloak.

SPIDERMAN MASK

You could, of course, be really creative and invent and dress up as your own superhero, and create your own adventures with completely new heroes and villains!

WORLD OF SORCERY

October 31st is better known to us all as Halloween, the night when all kinds of strange, supernatural things take place. Traditionally, on this night witches and wizards and all kinds of other mysterious creatures get together to have fun and make mischief. If you want to join in their fun and parties, you'll have to look pretty convincing not to be found out (and, in all probability, turned into stone!)

Witch

A witch is a woman who goes around in a long black skirt and cloak with a pointed hat, casting all kinds of spells with her magic wand and spell book. It's also a very easy look to create yourself.

> **The witch look:**
> long black skirt
> cloak
> pointed hat
> book of spells
> magic wand
> broomstick

Skirt

The easiest thing to do is to see if your mum has an old black skirt she'll let you borrow, and you can adapt it to fit. If not, you'll need to make a skirt from scratch. A good starting point is an old black-out curtain, or blanket. Or you could use an old bed sheet — you could legitimately call yourself a *white* witch if you wanted!

You will need:
Tape measure   Scissors
Tailors' chalk   Elastic
Cotton fabric   Needle and thread

Before you adapt your material, you'll need to take a couple of measurements: witches come in all shapes and sizes. Ask someone to measure you from your waist to your ankles, and then around your waist.

1. Double your waist measurement to find the width of the fabric needed. Add 3cm (1¼in) to your waist to ankle measurement to find the length of fabric needed.

2. With a tape measure and tailors' chalk transfer these measurements to the wrong side of the fabric to make a rectangle, and cut out the material.

3. Hem all along the bottom of the skirt (see p. 12).

4. Fold the rectangle in half, right sides together, and sew the two raw edges together with running stitches (see p. 10), making a neat seam.

5. Turn over the last raw edge at the top of the skirt by 2cm (¾in). Sew along the bottom of the turnover, leaving a gap of 4cm (1½in).

6. Thread the elastic through the gap and around the top hem. Knot the two ends of the elastic. Try on the skirt: if it's too tight or loose, adjust the length of the elastic. Sew up the gap.

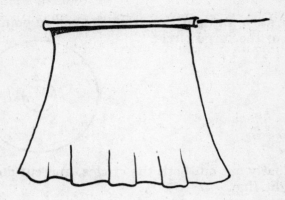

For a spooky additional touch, buy some cheap joke spiders and sew them to the front of the skirt (looping around their legs should secure them firmly).

Cloak

If you want to make a simple cloak, see p. 112.
If you'd like to make something more sophisticated, here's a neat plan for one.

You will need:	
Tape measure	Large piece of fabric
Tailors' chalk	Scissors
Compass *or* string and pencil	Needle and thread
	Brooch

1. Measure from your neck down to your knees.

2. Using tailors' chalk, draw a large circle on the fabric with a radius equal to the above measurement.

3. Draw a smaller circle in the middle 12cm (5in) across.

4. Draw a straight line from the centre point to the edge of the large circle.

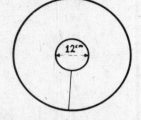

5. Neatly cut out both the circles, and cut down the straight line.

6. Hem the outer edge. Then turn under the edge of the inner circle and hem, leaving a gap to thread through the cloak tie.

7. Thread the ribbon, string or lace through the top hem and sew up the gap.

If you don't want to do this, you could use a brooch to hold the top of the cloak together.

Pointed hat

The traditional pointed witch's hat is really easy to make.

> *You will need:*
> Piece of black card (or white card and some black paint), 90cm (3ft) × 30cm (1ft)
> Pencil
> Compass
> Scissors
> Glue
> Silver foil

1. On the piece of card draw a semi-circle with a radius of 30cm (1ft) and a circle with a diameter of 30cm (1ft) with your compass on the point.

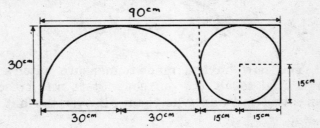

2. Cut out the two shapes — one semi-circular, the other a full circle.

3. Take the semi-circular piece of card and fold it around until one edge overlaps the other, making a cone.

4. Spread some glue on the inside of the overlapping edge, sticking the two surfaces together. Hold it firmly until it's dry.

5. Put the cone on your head. If it's too big, carefully cut around the bottom of the cone until it fits securely over your ears.

6. Place the cone in the centre of the circular piece of card and draw around it.

7. Draw a circle about 1cm (½in) in from the circle you've just drawn, and cut along the outer circle.

8. Score around the inner circle and, every 2cm (¾in) or so, cut a 'V' until it reaches the inner circle. Push the lips upwards.

9. Apply glue to the lips and place the cone over the top, pressing the lips to the inside of the cone until the glue dries.

10. You now have a made-to-measure witch's hat. For a final touch, cut out some stars and crescents from silver foil and glue them all over the hat.

Book of spells

We all know that witches have the ability to cast all kinds of evil and fiendish spells, don't we? Well, most of the witches I know also have really appalling memories: how many times have your witch friends turned your grandma into a frog and then promptly forgotten the spell to turn her back into a human being? The prudent witch, of course, always carries her book of spells wherever she goes!

The simplest way of making a spell book is to cheat by using an old hardback book you have lying around and making a cover for it.

You will need:

Hardback book	Pencil
Large (at least 25cm [10in] × 50cm [20in]) piece of thick black paper (spell books are *always* black!)	Scissors
	Sticky tape
	White felt-tip pen *or* typist's correction fluid
Ruler	

1. Open out your book and lay it on the piece of paper. Take a ruler and draw a straight line a few inches out from the edges of the book.

2. Cut along the line you've just drawn, cutting a diagonal line across each corner.

3. Fold the paper around the edge of the book, and, where it overlaps, fix a piece of sticky tape. BE CAREFUL NOT TO STICK IT TO THE BOOK ITSELF!

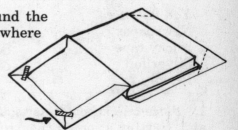

4. Close the book and trim the paper at the top and bottom of the spine.

5. Using a white felt-tip pen (failing that, typist's correction fluid is just as good), write on the cover something like 'SPELLS: any unauthorized person who tries to look in here will instantly turn into a donkey. BEWARE!'

Of course, if you're a perfectionist, you could make up your own spells and write them down in an exercise book (which you could then cover as above). This would be hard work and very time consuming, but you would be the life and soul of any party when trying out the spells on unsuspecting friends!

Magic wand

To help you cast your spells you will need a magic wand. These come in all shapes and sizes: at its most simple, a wand can just be a short stick, but here are a couple of better ideas:

The standard-issue witch's wand
This one is really very easy and quite effective.

You will need:	
Newspaper	Card
Sticky tape	Scissors
Silver foil	Glue
Pencil	

1. Place one sheet of newspaper on top of the other and, starting at one corner, roll them up as tightly as possible.

2. When you get to the other corner, tape the edge down to form a fairly sturdy 'tube'.

3. Now take the piece of silver foil and wrap it round the whole tube, taping down the edges with sticky tape.

4. Draw a star on the card. Cut it out and cover it with a small piece of leftover silver foil. Glue the star to the end of the wand.

There you are! Just wave the wand about a little bit and try out a few spells. New wands, you see, are just like new shoes — they have to be worn in.

The super-wand

Whilst sufficient for simple magic, the standard-issue wand is hardly powerful enough to turn Uncle Fred into a rhino! Much more effective is this super-wand. It's a little bit more complicated, though, so you may need some help from your parents. Alternatively, you could strap a pencil torch on to a stick with sticky tape and cover the whole thing with silver foil.

You will need:
- 2 pieces of covered wire, 37cm (15in) long
- 1.5-volt light bulb and holder (any shape as long as the holder has 'ears' at the side for fixing)
- Piece of plastic tubing, 30cm (1ft) long × 1cm (½in) in diameter
- 1.5-volt battery
- Sticky tape
- Silver foil
- Pencil
- Cardboard
- Scissors
- Glue

---

1. Fix the two pieces of wire to the connectors of the light-bulb holder.

2. Pass them through the plastic tube so that they poke through the other end, and push the holder down until it is fixed securely on the end of the tube.

3. Fix one piece of wire to each end of the battery. The firmer the fix, the better: soldering is the best way, but it's quite safe to use sticky tape.

4. Push the battery into the other end of the tube.

5. Now screw the light bulb in: it should light up. If it doesn't, one of the four connections has come adrift (unless, of course, the battery or bulb is 'dead').

IMPORTANT POINT: It's quite safe to unscrew the bulb each time you want to use it, because the voltage used is so low. DON'T EVEN THINK of doing this to normal mains light bulbs because it's *very* dangerous. Even witches are safety conscious where electricity is concerned!

6. Assuming the bulb worked OK, take it out again and cover the rod in silver foil as before, this time making certain that the foil doesn't come into contact with the terminals of the bulb holder.

7. Finally, make a star out of cardboard and cover it with silver foil and fix it behind the bulb holder. Then screw the bulb in again and there you have it – an illuminated magic wand – great for those dark halloween parties.

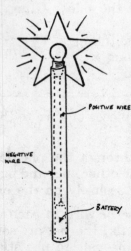

Broomstick

Witches don't need cars, trains, bikes or aeroplanes to get around, you know. They have something much more effective: a broomstick! Whenever a witch has to go down to the shops you'll never catch her waiting for a number 9 bus when she can just jump on her broomstick, utter a spell, and fly off into the sky!

You will need:
Old broom handle (or piece of doweling rod)
Black paint
Twigs
Piece of string at least 60cm (24in) in length

1. Take the broom handle and paint it black. Let it dry off.

2. Go into the garden or local park and find about 10 thin twigs. 'Straighten' them out snapping off any off-shoots that protrude too far outwards.

3. Put the twigs in a bundle, and pass the broom handle about 15cm (6in) into the middle of the bundle.

4. Take a piece of string and tie a single knot around the top end of the whole bundle as tightly as you can. Now tightly wind the rest of the string gradually moving down to the bottom of the bundle.

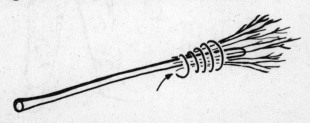

Dressed in your pointed hat, and your long black skirt and cloak, and armed with your wand, spell book and broomstick, no one will be able to tell that you're only impersonating a witch . . . or are you?!

Wizard

A wizard looks very similar to a witch, really. So most of the suggestions described above — the cloak, wand, and spell book — are all equally applicable to the wizard. The obvious exception is the skirt: you won't find too many wizards wearing one of those!

Trousers

Creating a pair of trousers for the wizard is quite simple. The most important thing about them is that they must be black and have lots of magic symbols painted over them.

If you have an old pair of trousers to convert, just dye them black, and cover them with stars, crescents and other magic symbols. It's probably not a good idea to stick or sew silver foil on to the trousers, as this is most likely to crinkle up and tear. The best thing to use is gold and silver fabric paint.

Hat

The wizard's hat is quite similar to the witch's hat. The only difference is that it has no rim.

Making a wizard's hat is very much like making a pointed hat (see p. 58). The only difference is that the wizard's hat, instead of being covered in a shiny fabric and ribbons, is painted black and covered in stars and crescents. These *can* be cut from silver foil or milk-bottle tops and glued straight on to the surface.

Ghost

Ghosts come in all shapes and sizes, but the simplest is the traditional pantomime ghost, which is basically a big white sheet that moves about!

Bed sheets are ideal for this. All you have to do is put one over your head, making sure that it covers your whole body, then move about waving your hands: you'll now look like a great big white blob! If you like, you can modify this appearance by decorating the sheet. Here are a few ideas.

Decorating the sheet

You will need:
Bed sheet
Pencil
Fabric paint
Paintbrush
Needle and thread
Glue
2 table-tennis balls
Black wool
2 springs *or* thin wire
Scissors
Cardboard
Carrot

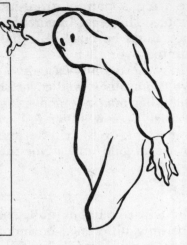

1. Work out where the face should be. This is easy to do. Put the sheet on, then take a pencil and draw around the outside of your own face.

2. Remove the sheet and decorate the sheet face. Try drawing or painting a ghostly face.

3. Alternatively sew or glue on the parts of the face. For example, make a pair of eyes on springs from two table-tennis balls. Simple paint an eye on the front of each one. For additional effect, glue a few pieces of black wool around the edges, to give the effect of eyelashes.

4. Then glue a spring to the back of each eye. If you don't have a spring, you can easily make one out of some strong, thin wire. Simply wrap the wire tightly around a tubular object, such as a pencil, and then slide it off.

5. Cut out a small circle of white card, and glue the other end of the spring to that. If you hold the circular card at the edges and wobble it around, the eye should also wobble around.

6. Sew the white card to the sheet where the eyes should go. Use as thick a thread as you can find, and make the stitches as uneven as possible. This will make it look like a grotesque scar!

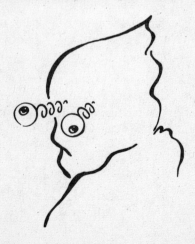

7. For the nose, why not use something like an old carrot?

8. Instead of making a mouth, draw on a big mouth, and then sew around it, using big, ugly stitches like you did for the eyes.

9. For a fancy-dress party, you could dab some luminous paint over the ghost's 'face'. Luminous paint is most commonly used for the numbers on clock faces so that they shine in the dark.

Obviously these are only a few ideas. How many other really weird, spooky ideas can you come up with?

MONSTERS AND VILLAINS

Dressing up as monsters and villains can be great fun for all kinds of party games. They're especially good, too, for sneaking up behind your friends and giving them the biggest fright of their lives! Here are a few looks that you can create, although there are numerous others that you might like to work out for yourselves.

Frankenstein monster

The Frankenstein monster was created by Mary Shelley in a novel of the same name. However, it was the early days of cinema that made him truly famous. In the story, the monster was created by a mad doctor called Frankenstein from pieces of other humans! So, in appearing like the monster, you should be trying to look as if *you've* been constructed from lots of old bits!

The key to the look is in the make-up. The clothes you need are not too important, although they should be really big and black and a bit tatty.

The Frankenstein look:
make-up
headband with nuts and bolts
baggy black or grey suit
boots

Make-up

You will need:
Make-up
Black thread
Scissors
Glue

1. Begin by making your face as white as you possibly can (see p. 20). Then take some black make-up and smear it very heavily around the edges of your eyes.

2. You can make a really hideous scar – a good one would go right across the forehead – by just drawing it on (see p. 22). However, a nice effect is to draw on the cut, and then to fix on some stitches using real black thread. To do this, take some thread and cut it into 25mm (1in) segments: fifteen pieces should be enough. Then, using some glue, carefully fix the threads across the scar. If this is done well, it can look really effective!

WARNING: Be sure not to use really strong 'super-glues', or you may find yourself with permanent scars!

Bolt

A feature that appears in popular images of the monster – although not in any of the films or books – is a bolt through the head or neck.

You will need:
Thick 10cm- (4in-) long nut and bolt (the rustier the better)
Super glue
Junior hacksaw
Plastic headband
Blu-Tack *or* Plasticine
Paint
Paintbrush

1. Screw the nut on to the bolt. When it's a few inches down the thread, glue it firmly in place with the super glue.

2. Saw the nut and bolt in half. You'll need a hacksaw to do this, so it may be better to ask an adult to help. If you're going to do it yourself, tell an adult first, because hacksaws can give nasty cuts if not used properly.

3. Take the headband and apply some super glue to one end, and to the end of one half of the bolt. If you do not have any super glue, use Blu-Tack or Plasticine to hold it in place. Hold the band and the bolt until they're dry. Do the same on the other side.

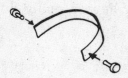

4. Paint the band a colour to match your own hair. Wear it around the back of your head and in your hair so that you appear to have a bolt going right through your head!

If you can obtain a smaller headband that fits tightly around the back of your neck, you can achieve the effect of a bolt passing right through the neck.

In fact this technique can be used to create a number of other illusions. Why not, for example, fix a tomahawk (see p. 85), or a knife to a headband? Here are a few ideas:

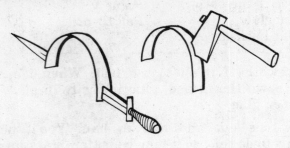

Suit

Clothes should be large and, if possible, black and tatty. If you can get hold of an adult's old jacket, this would do nicely. Simply put on a lot of layers of clothing before wearing the jacket.

You could also make some shoulder pads by taking some old pieces of material and folding them until they are about 15cm (6in) square. Place them over your shoulders before putting on the jacket. Your shoulders will now appear really huge!

Boots

The traditional monster also wears large boots, several sizes too big. Again, try to get hold of a pair of adult's old shoes that are many sizes too big for you. Put on loads of pairs of socks and stuff the ends of the boots with newspaper until they fit.

All you have to do now is to stomp around in a very stiff way, with a zombie-like expression on your face!

Dracula

The Dracula look:
hair parting
black cloak
fangs
a pale face

The parting

You will need: Make-up

If you cannot make your hair part correctly, draw the parting on your forehead using some make-up that closely matches the colour of your hair.

Cloak

You will need:
Black cotton fabric   Safety pin *or* brooch

Wrap the fabric around your neck and secure it at the front with the safety pin or brooch.

Fangs

Dracula fangs are widely available from joke shops or toy shops (if you haven't still got the ones you found in last year's Christmas crackers!). If you don't want to buy Dracula fangs, here is a very simple way of making them.

> *You will need:*
> Pencil
> White card, 5cm (2in) square
> Scissors
> Paperclip
> Disinfectant
> Sticky tape

1. Draw out a couple of fangs on a piece of white card and cut them out.

2. Take a paperclip and open it out. Give it a quick wash in disinfectant (as it has to go in your mouth). Now bend it into the shape shown below:

3. Fix the fangs to the paperclip ends, using a small piece of sticky tape. Fit the whole thing into the top of your mouth between your lips and gums.

Pale face

The classic Dracula look, as he appeared in the early silent films, showed him with an extremely white face. This look is easy to achieve using white stage paint: simply apply it to the whole of your face, much in the same way as shown in making up the clown's face. Later films showed him with a less dramatic but still notably pale skin. This can be achieved just by using a regular pale foundation cream and talcum powder.

For a more striking effect, some joke shops or stage make-up shops sell luminous face cream. This looks just like white stage paint, but glows in the dark. That's dramatic!

BIZARRE NOTIONS

Here are a few really bizarre ideas! They're the kind of outfits that really get you noticed at fancy-dress parties! Have you ever thought of dressing up as a piece of fruit?! Or as a famous building?

Banana

Seriously, dressing up as a banana is not as crazy or as difficult as it may seem! The skin is made up out of four pieces of cardboard: two crescent shapes for the sides; and a front and a back. Arm holes and leg holes are cut out of each of the side pieces and a large hole for the face is cut out of the front.

You will need:
Tape measure
Pencil
Corrugated cardboard
Scissors
Masking tape
Yellow, black and green paint
Paintbrush

1. Mark up and cut out two rectangles of corrugated card. One piece should be 115cm (3ft 9in) × 52cm (21in); the other should be 90cm (3ft) × 52cm (21in). Make sure that the corrugations — the grooves in the card — run parallel to the shorter sides.

2. Take the larger piece of card and measure out a square 40cm (16in) × 40cm (16in) 7.5cm (3in) in from the bottom and the sides. Cut out the square.

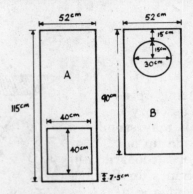

3. Take the smaller piece of card and measure out a circle with a diameter of 30cm (1ft), centred 30cm (1ft) from the top. Cut out the circle.

4. Gently curve both pieces of card lengthways. Take a piece of masking tape and stick the tops of both pieces together. Do this by cutting off 60cm (2ft) of the tape, sticking half of it over one edge, and folding the other half over the other edge.

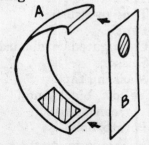

5. Repeat step 4 for the bottom ends. If you push both ends in at the same time, you will be able to create a crescent shape when viewed from the side.

6. Hold the crescent shape down on another piece of corrugated card and draw around it. Do this twice to create two identical crescents.

7. Mark out and cut a circle halfway along each crescent.

8. Fix the crescents to the side of the body using masking tape as in step 4.

9. You should now be able to fit the whole structure over your head and get your arms through the circles at the side. If any of the four holes are too small, now is the time to enlarge them.

10. The final step is to paint the banana. If you look at a real banana, you'll see that while it is nearly all yellow, there is always a black section at the top, where the banana joined the tree. You'll also notice that there are a few little black areas, or, if the banana isn't yet ripe, patches of green.

11. As a finishing touch, you could also wear yellow or pale green clothes underneath. You could even paint a pair of plimsoles with yellow fabric paint.

Empire State Building

We're now getting into very strange territory! Here are some very unusual ideas which are especially interesting if you're intending to go to a fancy-dress party. Remember, it's nearly always the unexpected that wins. There's no reason at all why you can't dress up as a famous building!

The Empire State Building is one of the most famous buildings in the world. And, believe it or not, as a piece of fancy dress, it's also fairly simple to build. The basic outline of the building looks like this (it's been a little simplified!).

You will need:
Tape measure
Pencil
Corrugated cardboard
Scissors
Grey, white and black paint (possible some black felt-tip pens)
Washing-up liquid bottle
Knitting needle *or* wire coat hanger
Masking tape, 5cm (2in) wide
Strong glue

Main body

The body can be made from two pieces of card.

1. Measure yourself from the top of your head to your ankles (call this measurement A). Then measure the distance from one shoulder to the other and add 7.5cm (3in) to this figure (call this measurement B). The main body of the building will be a box with the height of measurement A, and the width of measurement B.

2. Measure up and mark two pieces of card with a width slightly larger than twice B and a depth of A.

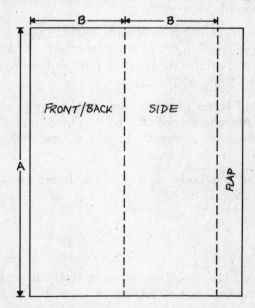

3. Cut along the outlines and score and fold along two lines (one at a width of B and the second a width of twice B) at 90 degrees. This will give you two sides and a 'lip' for fixing one to the other.

4. Before gluing them together it's a good idea to draw the design and cut the holes for the face and arms. Mark them, and cut them out so that the box will fit you comfortably.

5. Drawing and painting each window of the building individually would be an enormous task, so unless you have plenty of patience, just draw columns of black and white to give the impression of windows.

6. Liberally apply strong glue to the 'lips' of the card and fix the two pieces together. Hold them in place until they are dry. You may want to give some additional strength by running some masking tape down the inside of each joint.

7. Take another piece of card and mark out a square with sides the length of measurement B. Add a 5cm (2in) lip to each side. Cut it out and score and fold along the lines of the lip.

8. Spread some glue on each of the 'lips', and fit the square into the top of the body. Once again, you can give additional strength to the joints with masking tape.

9. Try on the 'body'. If any of the holes are too small, enlarge them.

Top

The top of the building is essentially a smaller box, with a rocket-shaped aerial at the tip.

1. The box should be about 30cm (1ft) high, and measurement B less 15cm (6in) square. So, take a piece of card and mark it out like this:

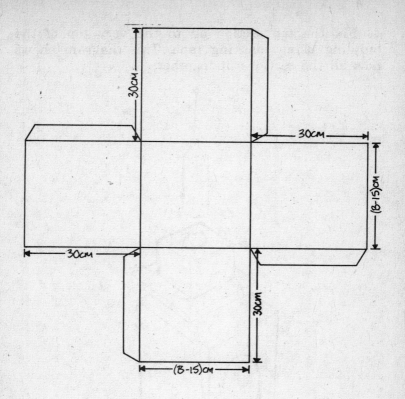

2. Cut it out, and score and fold the lines. Draw or paint the windows, as you did above, and when dry, apply glue to the 'lips' and hold them in place.

3. To make the aerial, the best instant solution is a washing-up liquid bottle! Paint the bottle white and glue it to the centre of the box. If you've kept the sprinkler (the bit at the top of the bottle), simply fix an old knitting needle in the top. Alternatively, open out a wire coat-hanger and place that in the top.

4. Fix the top section on to the very top of the building using masking tape. This diagram shows how all the sections fit together:

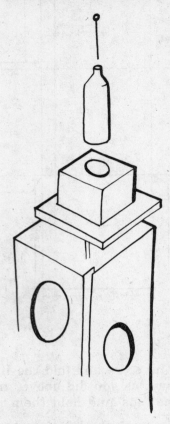

Finishing touches

Why not attempt one of the most famous images of the Empire State Building seen at the end of the film *King Kong*, where the huge gorilla climbs to the top of the building? If you have a cuddly toy gorilla, or something similar, fix it to the top of the building!